# Television Production Workbook

### NINTH EDITION

## Herbert Zettl

San Francisco State University

with Ronald J. Osgood, Indiana University

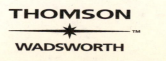

THOMSON

WADSWORTH

AUSTRALIA ■ BRAZIL ■ CANADA ■ MEXICO ■ SINGAPORE ■ SPAIN
UNITED KINGDOM ■ UNITED STATES

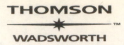

*Television Production Workbook,* **Ninth Edition**

Herbert Zettl with Ronald J. Osgood

*Publisher:* Holly J. Allen

*Assistant Editor:* Darlene Amidon-Brent

*Editorial Assistant:* Sarah Allen

*Senior Technology Project Manager:* Jeanette Wiseman

*Senior Marketing Manager:* Mark Orr

*Marketing Communications Manager:* Shemika Britt

*Marketing Assistant:* Alexandra Tran

*Project Manager, Editorial Production:* Christy Krueger

*Art Director:* Maria Epes

*Print/Media Buyer:* Lisa Claudeanos

*Production Service:* Ideas to Images

*Cover and Text Designer:* Gary Palmatier, Ideas to Images

*Art Editor:* Gary Palmatier, Ideas to Images

*Photo Researcher:* Roberta Broyer

*Copy Editor:* Elizabeth von Radics

*Compositor:* Ideas to Images

*Printer:* Thomson West

*Photo Credits*

Edward Aiona: 3, 4, 31 (Ex. 11), 38, 44, 46, 47 (Ex. 2c & 2d), 48 (Ex. 3), 63, 64, 89 (nos. 37–39), 90 (nos. 40–42), 91 (nos. 43–45), 122, 124 (Ex. 3a & 3b), 125, 131, 133, 150–153, 187 (Ex. 1a & 1c), 188, 189, 190 (Ex. 1k & 1l), 191

Broadcast and Electronic Communication Arts Department at San Francisco State University: 194–195 (Ex. 1)

Frezzi Energy Systems: 54 (no. 33)

Thomson/Grass Valley: 90 (Ex. 1), 92 (Ex. 8, top), 93 (Ex. 9, top), 94 (Ex. 10, top), 96 (Ex. 1)

Lowel-Light Mfg., Inc.: 54 (nos. 32 & 37)

John Veltri: 113, 114

MCI: 82 (Ex. 6)

Mole-Richardson Co.: 54 (nos. 30, 31, 35, 36 & 38)

Chris Rozales: 30 (Ex. 9)

Selco Products Company: 81 (Ex. 5)

Herbert Zettl: all other photos

ISBN 0-534-64728-6

**Thomson Higher Education**
**10 Davis Drive**
**Belmont, CA 94002-3098**
**USA**

For more information about our products, contact us at:
**Thomson Learning Academic Resource Center**
**1-800-423-0563**

For permission to use material from this text or product, submit a request online at *http://www.thomsonrights.com*. Any additional questions about permissions can be submitted by e-mail to *thomsonrights@thomson.com*.

*To all the students using this workbook, with the best wishes for success*

# Contents

# Preface

The basic purpose of the *Television Production Workbook,* Ninth Edition, is to facilitate students' learning of the increasingly complex world of television production and to give the instructor a standard instrument with which to measure and assess student progress. I find the *Workbook* especially valuable as a diagnostic tool. The initial resistance to some of the *Workbook* exercises usually dissipates quickly when students realize how much they actually don't know about the more complex production tools and processes. Even students in my advanced production courses are often surprised to find considerable weaknesses in areas that they considered their production specialty, and they usually welcome the opportunity to brush up on their deficiencies.

The chapters in this edition of the *Workbook* correspond to those of the *Television Production Handbook,* Ninth Edition, without necessarily being tied to them. Students should be encouraged to solve the assigned *Workbook* problems at least initially without the use of the *Handbook*. This way the results will reflect a more accurate picture of each student's knowledge of television production; it will also provide him or her with a more realistic guide for further study. When used in conjunction with *Zettl's VideoLab 3.0* DVD-ROM, the *Workbook* can serve as a handy extension of the disc's quizzes and skills testing. Eventually, students must translate the written exercises into actual studio and field production experiences. I hope that the *Workbook* will make such a translation as painless and effective as possible.

The *Workbook* is laid out for ease of use and optimal student learning. Here are some of its main features:

▶ Each chapter begins with a review of key terms that tests the understanding of that chapter's basic terminology.

▶ The middle section of each chapter offers a variety of objective questions, including illustrations that need to be analyzed. The aim is to help students with the effective application of the most appropriate production principles.

▶ Each chapter ends with a true/false Review Quiz.

▶ All objective questions can be answered by filling in numbered "bubbles." This design is intended to minimize ambiguity in answering and maximize speed and accuracy in evaluating. Because each bubble is assigned a specific number, the design lends itself readily to computer scoring. The numerical scale also facilitates the setting of achievement standards when grading.

▶ A number of problems require multiple answers, which means that students should fill in two or more bubbles. Whenever such multiple answers are not obvious, the instructions indicate "Fill in two bubbles" or "Multiple answers are possible."

▶ If you use the *Workbook* in conjunction with *Zettl's VideoLab 3.0* DVD-ROM, students can follow up the *Workbook* problems with relevant interactive exercises on the disc. Such a combination of testing and interactive study makes the learning process less abstract while reinforcing the information in the *Handbook*.

▶ The Problem-solving Applications at the end of each chapter require subjective answers. This section gives students the opportunity to put their knowledge into a realistic context and seek creative solutions to a variety of common production problems. You are encouraged to add other such production problems that are specific to your own requirements and production environment.

▶ The floor plan grids and storyboard sheets at the back of the book can be used to solve some of the subjective problems in the *Workbook*. You are encouraged to photocopy them so that students can use them for a variety of preproduction tasks that are not part of the *Workbook* exercises.

You will find that the problems differ considerably in degree of difficulty. Some are designed simply for quick recall; others require a more careful evaluation of the possible solutions to the problems. I usually inform students of these differences and encourage them not to get careless, especially when they find the answers to be quite obvious.

## ACKNOWLEDGMENTS

Again, my thanks to the people at Wadsworth Publishing Company who insist on a workbook that is as efficient to use as it is effective for student learning. I am most grateful to my colleague, Dr. Ronald Osgood, who helped polish some of the existing *Workbook* problems and also wrote a number of new ones. Dr. Robin Riley and Rudi Benzler deserve much credit for scrutinizing and answering all problems in the *Workbook* to make sure that they are answerable and free of ambiguities. I am especially indebted to my former colleagues and students who helped me with formulating the various problems and doubled as on-camera talent.

I was privileged to work again with the "A-team" that helped with the Ninth Edition of the *Television Production Handbook:* Holly Allen and Darlene Amidon-Brent of Thomson; Gary Palmatier and Robaire Ream of Ideas to Images, who did the design, page layout, and artwork; Elizabeth von Radics, copy editor; and Ed Aiona, master photographer.

Finally, I owe a big thank-you to my wife, Erika, who as a longtime classroom teacher, administrator, and educational consultant taught me how to clarify and objectify the answers without impinging on the students' creativity.

# 1 The Television Production Process

## REVIEW OF KEY TERMS

*Match each term with its appropriate definition by filling in the corresponding bubble.*

1. system
2. EFP
3. tapeless system
4. camcorder
5. ENG
6. switcher
7. studio talkback
8. intercom
9. line-out

**A.** The signal that carries the video or audio output for broadcast or recording.

A
○ ○ ○ ○ ○
1 2 3 4 5
○ ○ ○ ○
6 7 8 9

**B.** A public address system from the control room to the studio.

B
○ ○ ○ ○ ○
1 2 3 4 5
○ ○ ○ ○
6 7 8 9

**C.** The interrelationship of various elements and processes in which the proper functioning of each element is dependent on all others.

C
○ ○ ○ ○ ○
1 2 3 4 5
○ ○ ○ ○
6 7 8 9

**D.** A panel with rows of buttons that allows the selection and assembly of various video sources through a variety of transition devices.

D
○ ○ ○ ○ ○
1 2 3 4 5
○ ○ ○ ○
6 7 8 9

PAGE
TOTAL [    ]

| 1. system | 4. camcorder | 7. studio talkback |
|-----------|--------------|---------------------|
| 2. EFP | 5. ENG | 8. intercom |
| 3. tapeless system | 6. switcher | 9. line-out |

**E.** An alternative to videotape recording and playback that uses computer storage devices exclusively.

E  ○ ○ ○ ○ ○  
  1 2 3 4 5  
  ○ ○ ○ ○  
  6 7 8 9

**F.** Television production outside the studio that is usually shot for postproduction.

F  ○ ○ ○ ○ ○  
  1 2 3 4 5  
  ○ ○ ○ ○  
  6 7 8 9

**G.** Television production that covers daily news events and is usually transmitted live or after immediate postproduction.

G  ○ ○ ○ ○ ○  
  1 2 3 4 5  
  ○ ○ ○ ○  
  6 7 8 9

**H.** A portable television camera with the VCR attached or built into it to form a single unit.

H  ○ ○ ○ ○ ○  
  1 2 3 4 5  
  ○ ○ ○ ○  
  6 7 8 9

**I.** A communications system used by production and technical personnel.

I  ○ ○ ○ ○ ○  
  1 2 3 4 5  
  ○ ○ ○ ○  
  6 7 8 9

PAGE TOTAL [ ]

SECTION TOTAL [ ]

## REVIEW OF THE TELEVISION SYSTEM

**1.** Identify each of the major elements of the basic television system by filling in the corresponding bubble.

**a.** VTR          **d.** TV receiver sound          **f.** microphone

**b.** TV receiver image          **e.** video signal          **g.** audio signal

**c.** TV camera

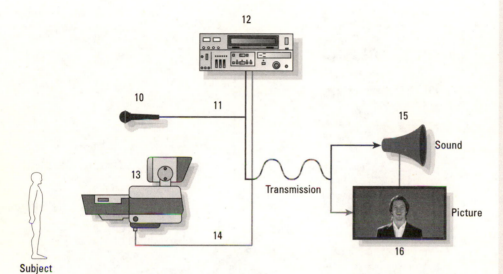

12

10          11

15  Sound

13

Transmission

Picture

14

16

Subject

**1a** ○ ○ ○ ○
10  11  12  13
○ ○ ○
14  15  16

**1b** ○ ○ ○ ○
10  11  12  13
○ ○ ○
14  15  16

**1c** ○ ○ ○ ○
10  11  12  13
○ ○ ○
14  15  16

**1d** ○ ○ ○ ○
10  11  12  13
○ ○ ○
14  15  16

**1e** ○ ○ ○ ○
10  11  12  13
○ ○ ○
14  15  16

**1f** ○ ○ ○ ○
10  11  12  13
○ ○ ○
14  15  16

**1g** ○ ○ ○ ○
10  11  12  13
○ ○ ○
14  15  16

PAGE
TOTAL

**2.** Identify each major component of the expanded television system by filling in the corresponding bubble.

**a.** audio monitor speaker

**b.** videotape recorder

**c.** CCUs 1 and 2

**d.** audio console

**e.** home TV receiver

**f.** video switcher

**g.** transmitter

**h.** line monitor

**i.** cameras 1 and 2

**j.** preview monitors

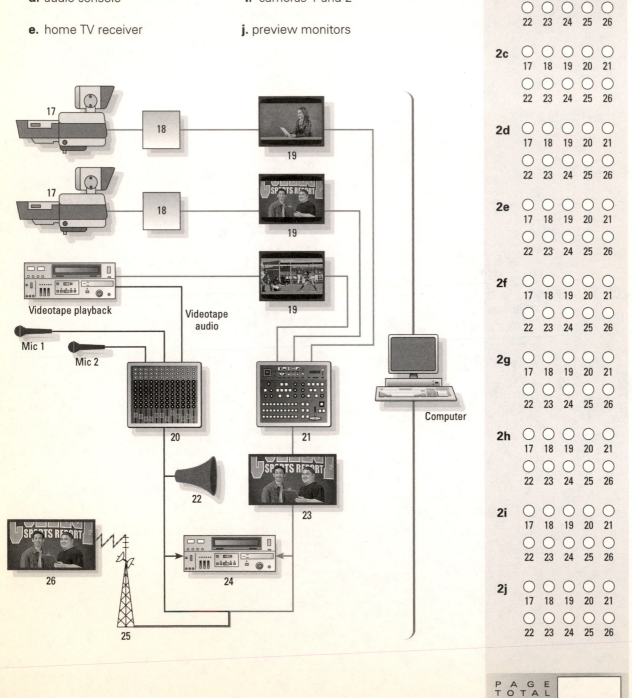

Videotape playback

Videotape audio

Mic 1

Mic 2

Computer

| | 2a | 17 | 18 | 19 | 20 | 21 |
| | | 22 | 23 | 24 | 25 | 26 |
| | 2b | 17 | 18 | 19 | 20 | 21 |
| | | 22 | 23 | 24 | 25 | 26 |
| | 2c | 17 | 18 | 19 | 20 | 21 |
| | | 22 | 23 | 24 | 25 | 26 |
| | 2d | 17 | 18 | 19 | 20 | 21 |
| | | 22 | 23 | 24 | 25 | 26 |
| | 2e | 17 | 18 | 19 | 20 | 21 |
| | | 22 | 23 | 24 | 25 | 26 |
| | 2f | 17 | 18 | 19 | 20 | 21 |
| | | 22 | 23 | 24 | 25 | 26 |
| | 2g | 17 | 18 | 19 | 20 | 21 |
| | | 22 | 23 | 24 | 25 | 26 |
| | 2h | 17 | 18 | 19 | 20 | 21 |
| | | 22 | 23 | 24 | 25 | 26 |
| | 2i | 17 | 18 | 19 | 20 | 21 |
| | | 22 | 23 | 24 | 25 | 26 |
| | 2j | 17 | 18 | 19 | 20 | 21 |
| | | 22 | 23 | 24 | 25 | 26 |

PAGE TOTAL

3. Match each system element with its appropriate function by filling in the corresponding bubble.

(27) cameras          (31) line monitor       (34) audio console

(28) preview monitors   (32) microphones      (35) CCUs

(29) TV receiver        (33) switcher          (36) VTR

(30) audio monitor speaker

**a.** To convert what we hear into electrical signals.

3a  ○ ○ ○ ○ ○
   27 28 29 30 31
   ○ ○ ○ ○ ○
   32 33 34 35 36

**b.** To record video and audio signals on a videotape.

3b  ○ ○ ○ ○ ○
   27 28 29 30 31
   ○ ○ ○ ○ ○
   32 33 34 35 36

**c.** To control the picture quality of the television cameras.

3c  ○ ○ ○ ○ ○
   27 28 29 30 31
   ○ ○ ○ ○ ○
   32 33 34 35 36

**d.** To control the audio quality of the various audio inputs.

3d  ○ ○ ○ ○ ○
   27 28 29 30 31
   ○ ○ ○ ○ ○
   32 33 34 35 36

**e.** To convert what we see into electrical signals.

3e  ○ ○ ○ ○ ○
   27 28 29 30 31
   ○ ○ ○ ○ ○
   32 33 34 35 36

**f.** To translate the broadcast signals into pictures and sound.

3f  ○ ○ ○ ○ ○
   27 28 29 30 31
   ○ ○ ○ ○ ○
   32 33 34 35 36

PAGE TOTAL [          ]

**g.** To display the pictures supplied by the various video sources.

**3g**  ○ ○ ○ ○ ○
27 28 29 30 31
○ ○ ○ ○ ○
32 33 34 35 36

**h.** To display the line-out pictures.

**3h**  ○ ○ ○ ○ ○
27 28 29 30 31
○ ○ ○ ○ ○
32 33 34 35 36

**i.** To reproduce the line-out sound.

**3i**  ○ ○ ○ ○ ○
27 28 29 30 31
○ ○ ○ ○ ○
32 33 34 35 36

**j.** To select video inputs.

**3j**  ○ ○ ○ ○ ○
27 28 29 30 31
○ ○ ○ ○ ○
32 33 34 35 36

PAGE
TOTAL

SECTION
TOTAL

## REVIEW OF STUDIOS, MASTER CONTROL, AND SUPPORT AREAS

1. Match each term with its appropriate definition by filling in the corresponding bubble.

(37) dimmer control board

(38) control room

(39) log

(40) master control

(41) wall jacks

(42) set dressing

(43) program retrieval

(44) line monitor

a. The devices that enable microphone cables and intercoms to be connected in the studio.

**1a** ○ ○ ○ ○
37  38  39  40
○ ○ ○ ○
41  42  43  44

b. Used to regulate the intensity of studio lights.

**1b** ○ ○ ○ ○
37  38  39  40
○ ○ ○ ○
41  42  43  44

c. A video monitor that is located in the control room and carries the line-out video for broadcast or recording.

**1c** ○ ○ ○ ○
37  38  39  40
○ ○ ○ ○
41  42  43  44

d. Items, such as plants or pictures, used as part of a studio set.

**1d** ○ ○ ○ ○
37  38  39  40
○ ○ ○ ○
41  42  43  44

e. A separate room adjacent to the studio, where all production activities are coordinated during the show.

**1e** ○ ○ ○ ○
37  38  39  40
○ ○ ○ ○
41  42  43  44

PAGE TOTAL [      ]

**f.** The second-by-second list of every program aired on a particular day.

**1f** ○ ○ ○ ○
37 38 39 40
○ ○ ○ ○
41 42 43 44

**g.** The nerve center for all telecasts; oversees technical quality of all program material.

**1g** ○ ○ ○ ○
37 38 39 40
○ ○ ○ ○
41 42 43 44

**h.** The selection, ordering, and airing of all program material.

**1h** ○ ○ ○ ○
37 38 39 40
○ ○ ○ ○
41 42 43 44

PAGE TOTAL

SECTION TOTAL

Course No. _____  Date _____  Name _____

## REVIEW QUIZ

*Mark the following statements as true or false by filling in the bubbles in the*
***T*** *(for true) or* ***F*** *(for false) column.*

|   |   | T | F |
|---|---|---|---|
| **1.** | The switcher allows instantaneous editing. | ○ 45 | ○ 46 |
| **2.** | In the television studio, we use spotlights and floodlights. | ○ 47 | ○ 48 |
| **3.** | Memory sticks and cards can be used to record brief video segments. | ○ 49 | ○ 50 |
| **4.** | The primary function of the C.G. is to enhance picture quality. | ○ 51 | ○ 52 |
| **5.** | The microphone converts sound into an electrical signal. | ○ 53 | ○ 54 |
| **6.** | Linear editing is copying shots onto another videotape in a specific order. | ○ 55 | ○ 56 |
| **7.** | We need at least two VTRs for nonlinear postproduction editing. | ○ 57 | ○ 58 |
| **8.** | With nonlinear editing you edit directly from the source tapes to the edit master tape. | ○ 59 | ○ 60 |
| **9.** | All audio consoles can select the signals from various incoming audio sources and control sound volume. | ○ 61 | ○ 62 |
| **10.** | Digital graphics generators can produce screen images without the aid of a television camera. | ○ 63 | ○ 64 |

SECTION TOTAL ☐

© 2006 Thomson Wadsworth

*Think through each production problem and consider the various options.*
*Then pick the most effective solution and justify your choice.*

1. List in any order the major components (equipment) of the expanded television system that will allow you to produce and select optimal pictures from three studio cameras, produce optimal sound from four microphones, and videotape and simultaneously transmit the signals to a television receiver. Now order these components and connect them with lines that show the basic signal flow from cameras, microphones, and the various video and audio selections to the videotape recorder and the home television receiver.

2. List the components of a linear videotape editing system that permits a dissolve, then draw a diagram that shows the basic signal flow for these components.

3. What system elements are incorporated into a single camcorder? What are some of the advantages and the disadvantages of the camcorder system compared with those of the expanded television system?

4. What exactly distinguishes ENG from EFP?

5. You have been asked to convert an office complex into a simple television studio. List several important physical characteristics that need to be considered to make the room effective as a studio.

6. List two alternative tapeless recording options and describe the advantages and the disadvantages of each.

# 2 Analog and Digital Television

## REVIEW OF KEY TERMS

*Match each term with its appropriate definition by filling in the corresponding bubble.*

| | | |
|---|---|---|
| 1. progressive scanning | 4. field | 7. HDTV |
| 2. streaming | 5. frame | 8. compression |
| 3. downloading | 6. interlaced scanning | |

**A.** A system in which the electron beam starts scanning line 1, then line 2, then line 3, and so forth until all lines are scanned.

A
○ ○ ○ ○
1  2  3  4
○ ○ ○ ○
5  6  7  8

**B.** The transfer of files sent in data packets.

B
○ ○ ○ ○
1  2  3  4
○ ○ ○ ○
5  6  7  8

**C.** A television standard with at least twice the picture detail of standard television.

C
○ ○ ○ ○
1  2  3  4
○ ○ ○ ○
5  6  7  8

**D.** The temporary rearrangement or elimination of redundant picture information for easier storage and signal transport.

D
○ ○ ○ ○
1  2  3  4
○ ○ ○ ○
5  6  7  8

**E.** The scanning of all odd-numbered scanning lines and the subsequent scanning of all even-numbered lines.

E
○ ○ ○ ○
1  2  3  4
○ ○ ○ ○
5  6  7  8

PAGE
TOTAL [       ]

| 1. progressive scanning | 4. field | 7. HDTV |
| 2. streaming | 5. frame | 8. compression |
| 3. downloading | 6. interlaced scanning | |

**F.** Delivering and receiving digital video as continuous data.

F
○ ○ ○ ○
1 2 3 4
○ ○ ○ ○
5 6 7 8

**G.** A complete interlaced scanning cycle.

G
○ ○ ○ ○
1 2 3 4
○ ○ ○ ○
5 6 7 8

**H.** One-half of a complete scanning cycle, with two of them necessary for a complete television frame.

H
○ ○ ○ ○
1 2 3 4
○ ○ ○ ○
5 6 7 8

PAGE
TOTAL

SECTION
TOTAL

## REVIEW OF ANALOG AND DIGITAL TELEVISION

*Select the correct answers and fill in the bubbles with the corresponding numbers.*

1. The four major steps of digitizing an analog signal are (9) *quantizing* (10) *analyzing* (11) *aliasing* (12) *antialiasing* (13) *compression* (14) *sampling* (15) *scanning* (16) *digital-to-analog conversion* (17) *coding.* **(Fill in four bubbles.)**

   **1** ○ ○ ○ ○ ○
       9  10  11  12  13
   ○ ○ ○ ○
   14  15  16  17

2. The aspect ratio for wide-screen HDTV is (18) *4 × 3* (19) *16 × 9* (20) *16 × 4.*

   **2** ○ ○ ○
     18   19   20

3. The standard television (STV) format is (21) *4 × 3* (22) *9 × 3* (23) *16 × 9.*

   **3** ○ ○ ○
     21   22   23

4. One of the major advantages of digital television is that (24) *it still uses analog signals* (25) *its picture does not deteriorate over numerous generations* (26) *it always uses interlaced scanning.*

   **4** ○ ○ ○
     24   25   26

5. The two operational DTV systems are (27) *1080i* (28) *1280p* (29) *720p.* **(Fill in two bubbles.)**

   **5** ○ ○ ○
     27   28   29

6. Standard NTSC television uses a (30) *progressive* (31) *interlaced* (32) *compressed* scanning system.

   **6** ○ ○ ○
     30   31   32

7. Digital television (33) *must use interlaced scanning* (34) *must use progressive scanning* (35) *can use either of the two systems.*

   **7** ○ ○ ○
     33   34   35

8. Which of the diagrams below represents most appropriately a digital signal?

   **8** ○ ○ ○
     36   37   38

(36)

(37)

(38)

SECTION TOTAL [   ]

## REVIEW QUIZ

Mark the following statements as true or false by filling in the bubbles in the
**T** (for true) or **F** (for false) column.

|  |  | T | F |
|---|---|---|---|
| **1.** | All flat-panel displays use the LCD system. | 1 ○ 39 | ○ 40 |
| **2.** | Assigning 0's and 1's to the sampled signal is part of antialiasing. | 2 ○ 41 | ○ 42 |
| **3.** | In the digital process, sampling must precede quantizing. | 3 ○ 43 | ○ 44 |
| **4.** | RBG are the basic primary colors of analog as well as digital television. | 4 ○ 45 | ○ 46 |
| **5.** | The most common compression standard for moving video is MPEG. | 5 ○ 47 | ○ 48 |
| **6.** | All digital video signals must be compressed before they can be recorded on videotape. | 6 ○ 49 | ○ 50 |
| **7.** | Analog recordings can tolerate more tape generations without noticeable loss than digital recordings. | 7 ○ 51 | ○ 52 |
| **8.** | Downloading allows you to view continuous data flow while the downloading is in progress. | 8 ○ 53 | ○ 54 |
| **9.** | The 16 × 9 aspect ratio is especially advantageous for showing wide-screen movies. | 9 ○ 55 | ○ 56 |
| **10.** | Digital signals are fluctuating signals that change continuously. | 10 ○ 57 | ○ 58 |

SECTION
TOTAL

## PROBLEM-SOLVING APPLICATIONS

1. You have been asked to plan the conversion of an existing analog studio to digital. You need to justify the decision because of the costs involved with the conversion. Some specific questions include: What makes the digital studio a better choice? What can the digital studio do that makes it better than the existing analog studio? State your case as convincingly as you can.

2. Your editor tells you that, contrary to sampling, which is an essential step in the digital process, compression is not compulsory. Do you agree with the editor? If so, why? If not, why not?

3. The same editor insists on all-digital equipment with as high a sampling ratio and as little compression as possible because your projects require extensive postproduction with a great number of complex effects. What is your reaction? Why?

4. Your friend, an ardent movie fan, is extremely happy about the new 16 × 9 aspect ratio because, according to him, it is especially well suited to playing back wide-screen movies. Do you agree with him? If so, why? If not, why not?

5. Your organization intends to deliver video content via the Internet. Some members of the organization want the content streamed, while others think that downloading is a better choice. List a few justifications for each argument.

6. Briefly list and explain the four-step process of digitization.

7. You have been asked to select one of the HDTV systems (720p or 1080i) for your television studio. Describe each and justify why you would choose one over the other.

# 3 The Television Camera

## REVIEW OF KEY TERMS

*Match each term with its appropriate definition by filling in the corresponding bubble.*

1. CCD
2. CCU
3. chrominance
4. camera chain
5. HDTV camera
6. resolution
7. pixel
8. luminance
9. signal-to-noise ratio
10. white balance

**A.** The smallest single imaging element.

A ① ② ③ ④ ⑤
6 7 8 9 10

**B.** The channel responsible for color.

B ① ② ③ ④ ⑤
6 7 8 9 10

**C.** The channel responsible for brightness.

C ① ② ③ ④ ⑤
6 7 8 9 10

**D.** A unit, separate from the camera, that is used to process signals coming from and going to the camera to ensure optimal television pictures.

D ① ② ③ ④ ⑤
6 7 8 9 10

PAGE TOTAL [      ]

| 1. CCD | 5. HDTV camera | 8. luminance |
| 2. CCU | 6. resolution | 9. signal-to-noise ratio |
| 3. chrominance | 7. pixel | 10. white balance |
| 4. camera chain | | |

**E.** The relation of the strength of the desired signal to the existing electronic interference.

E
○ ○ ○ ○ ○
1 2 3 4 5
○ ○ ○ ○ ○
6 7 8 9 10

**F.** The most common imaging device in color cameras.

F
○ ○ ○ ○ ○
1 2 3 4 5
○ ○ ○ ○ ○
6 7 8 9 10

**G.** A video camera that delivers superior resolution, color, and contrast.

G
○ ○ ○ ○ ○
1 2 3 4 5
○ ○ ○ ○ ○
6 7 8 9 10

**H.** The camera connected with the CCU, power supply, and sync generator.

H
○ ○ ○ ○ ○
1 2 3 4 5
○ ○ ○ ○ ○
6 7 8 9 10

**I.** The relative sharpness of the picture as measured by number of pixels.

I
○ ○ ○ ○ ○
1 2 3 4 5
○ ○ ○ ○ ○
6 7 8 9 10

**J.** Adjusting color circuits in a camera to produce a white color in lighting of various color temperatures.

J
○ ○ ○ ○ ○
1 2 3 4 5
○ ○ ○ ○ ○
6 7 8 9 10

PAGE TOTAL ☐

SECTION TOTAL ☐

*Chapter 3* — *The Television Camera*

## REVIEW OF BASIC CAMERA ELEMENTS AND FUNCTIONS

*Select the correct answers and fill in the bubbles with the corresponding numbers.*

**1.** The three basic parts of the camera are (11) *pedestal* (12) *viewfinder* (13) *VTR* (14) *imaging or pickup device* (15) *lens* (16) *tally light*. **(Fill in three bubbles.)**

**1**  ○ 11   ○ 12   ○ 13
   ○ 14   ○ 15   ○ 16

**2.** Fill in the bubbles whose numbers correspond with the camera elements shown in the following figure.

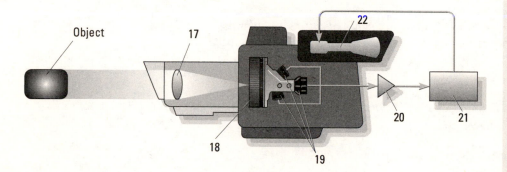

**a.** Transforms light into electric energy or video signals.

**2a**  ○ 17   ○ 18   ○ 19
    ○ 20   ○ 21   ○ 22

**b.** Amplifies video signals.

**2b**  ○ 17   ○ 18   ○ 19
    ○ 20   ○ 21   ○ 22

**c.** Converts signals back into visible screen images.

**2c**  ○ 17   ○ 18   ○ 19
    ○ 20   ○ 21   ○ 22

**d.** Processes video signal.

**2d**  ○ 17   ○ 18   ○ 19
    ○ 20   ○ 21   ○ 22

**e.** Gathers and transmits the light.

**2e**  ○ 17   ○ 18   ○ 19
    ○ 20   ○ 21   ○ 22

**f.** Splits the white light into red, green, and blue light beams.

**2f**  ○ 17   ○ 18   ○ 19
    ○ 20   ○ 21   ○ 22

**SECTION TOTAL** ＿＿＿＿＿

## REVIEW OF TELEVISION COLOR

*Select the correct answers and fill in the bubbles with the corresponding numbers.*

1. When all additive primaries are combined with equal intensity, we get
   (23) *black* (24) *white* (25) *yellow* light.

2. When red and green lights are mixed, we get (26) *yellow* (27) *brown*
   (28) *no* light.

3. The encoder combines the chrominance and the luminance into a single
   (29) *composite signal* (30) *component signal* (31) *Y/C signal.*

4. The three color attributes are (32) *hue* (33) *chromaticity* (34) *brightness*
   (35) *vibration* (36) *color temperature* (37) *saturation.* **(Fill in three bubbles.)**

5. Saturation is (38) *the richness or strength of a color* (39) *how light or dark a
   color appears* (40) *the color itself.*

6. The primary colors for television are (41) *RBY* (42) *RGB* (43) *Y/C.*

| | | | |
|---|---|---|---|
| **1** | ◯ 23 | ◯ 24 | ◯ 25 |
| **2** | ◯ 26 | ◯ 27 | ◯ 28 |
| **3** | ◯ 29 | ◯ 30 | ◯ 31 |
| **4** | ◯ 32 | ◯ 33 | ◯ 34 |
| | ◯ 35 | ◯ 36 | ◯ 37 |
| **5** | ◯ 38 | ◯ 39 | ◯ 40 |
| **6** | ◯ 41 | ◯ 42 | ◯ 43 |

SECTION TOTAL [ ]

## REVIEW OF ELECTRONIC CAMERA CHARACTERISTICS

*Match the functions of the camera chain and fill in the bubbles with the corresponding numbers.*

1. One of the CCU functions is to adjust (44) *the white level* (45) *the zoom level* (46) *focus* for optimal camera performance.

   1  ○ 44   ○ 45   ○ 46

2. The RCU functions as (47) *a CCU* (48) *the sync generator* (49) *remote lens control.*

   2  ○ 47   ○ 48   ○ 49

3. When using a separate RCU with an ENG/EFP camera, the RCU (50) *overrides the camera's automatic controls* (51) *operates with wireless controls.*

   3  ○ 50   ○ 51

4. The power supply of camcorders is normally a (52) *220-volt AC current* (53) *battery* (54) *power cable.*

   4  ○ 52   ○ 53   ○ 54

5. A professional video signal connector is called a (55) *BNC* (56) *XLR* (57) *mini plug.*

   5  ○ 55   ○ 56   ○ 57

6. To boost the video signal in low-light conditions, you use (58) *the gain control* (59) *image enhancers* (60) *a striped filter.*

   6  ○ 58   ○ 59   ○ 60

7. To minimize the blur of fast-moving objects, you need to use (61) *a low shutter speed* (62) *a high shutter speed* (63) *a moiré filter.*

   7  ○ 61   ○ 62   ○ 63

8. Television cameras have to be white-balanced to compensate for variations in (64) *their gain* (65) *voltage* (66) *color temperature of light.*

   8  ○ 64   ○ 65   ○ 66

SECTION TOTAL [　]

Mark the following statements as true or false by filling in the bubbles in the *T* (for true) or *F* (for false) column.

|  |  | T | F |
|---|---|---|---|

**1.** You can use a neutral density filter to reduce the intensity of bright light.

**1** ○ 67  ○ 68

**2.** Digital data can be transferred via a FireWire cable.

**2** ○ 69  ○ 70

**3.** A single pickup device delivers higher-quality color than using three image devices.

**3** ○ 71  ○ 72

**4.** A 10-meter cable is approximately 100 feet long.

**4** ○ 73  ○ 74

**5.** Digital signals are more prone to distortion than analog signals.

**5** ○ 75  ○ 76

**6.** An ever-increasing number of camcorders use flash drives or small hard drives as recording devices.

**6** ○ 77  ○ 78

**7.** Chrominance contains brightness information.

**7** ○ 79  ○ 80

**8.** 1080i is an HDTV resolution standard.

**8** ○ 81  ○ 82

**9.** White balance is important for ENG/EFP cameras but not for studio cameras.

**9** ○ 83  ○ 84

**10.** A high signal-to-noise ratio is desirable.

**10** ○ 85  ○ 86

SECTION TOTAL [ ]

## PROBLEM-SOLVING APPLICATIONS

1. List and describe four major features that distinguish a professional camcorder from a consumer camcorder.

2. When on an ENG assignment, you are forced to shoot in an extremely dark environment. There is no time to turn on any auxiliary lights, and your camcorder is not equipped with a camera light. What, if anything, can you do to produce visible images however noisy they may be?

3. When moving from outdoors to indoors, the field reporter tells you not to worry about white-balancing the camera again because the outside light of the foggy day seems to match the studio lighting anyway. What is your response? Why?

4. When watching a rehearsal of a dance company, the TD expresses concern because the dancers wear white leotards while performing a very fast number in front of a black background. Is the TD's concern justified? If so, why? If not, why not? What are your recommendations?

5. The TD tells the camera operator that a high shutter speed needs a considerable amount of light. What does the TD mean by *shutter speed*? When do you need a high shutter speed? How, if at all, is it related to light levels?

6. Draw and describe the parts of the camera chain and their primary functions.

# 4 Lenses

## REVIEW OF KEY TERMS

*Match each term with its appropriate definition by filling in the corresponding bubble.*

1. aperture
2. depth of field
3. fast lens
4. focal length

5. *f*-stop
6. field of view
7. normal lens

8. slow lens
9. wide-angle lens
10. zoom lens

**A.** The distance from the optical center of the lens to the front surface of the camera imaging device.

**B.** The general lens focal length that approximates the spatial relationships of normal vision.

**C.** The calibration on the lens indicating the diaphragm opening—and therefore the amount of light passing through the lens.

**D.** The area in which all objects, located at different distances from the camera, appear sharp and clear.

**E.** Variable-focal-length lens, which can change from a wide shot to a close-up and vice versa in one continuous movement.

A  ○ ○ ○ ○ ○
   1 2 3 4 5
   ○ ○ ○ ○ ○
   6 7 8 9 10

B  ○ ○ ○ ○ ○
   1 2 3 4 5
   ○ ○ ○ ○ ○
   6 7 8 9 10

C  ○ ○ ○ ○ ○
   1 2 3 4 5
   ○ ○ ○ ○ ○
   6 7 8 9 10

D  ○ ○ ○ ○ ○
   1 2 3 4 5
   ○ ○ ○ ○ ○
   6 7 8 9 10

E  ○ ○ ○ ○ ○
   1 2 3 4 5
   ○ ○ ○ ○ ○
   6 7 8 9 10

PAGE TOTAL [    ]

| 1. aperture | 5. *f*-stop | 8. slow lens |
|---|---|---|
| 2. depth of field | 6. field of view | 9. wide-angle lens |
| 3. fast lens | 7. normal lens | 10. zoom lens |
| 4. focal length | | |

**F.** Same as short-focal-length lens, which gives a broad view of a scene.

F
○ ○ ○ ○ ○
1 2 3 4 5
○ ○ ○ ○ ○
6 7 8 9 10

**G.** A lens that at its maximum aperture permits a relatively great amount of light to enter and pass through.

G
○ ○ ○ ○ ○
1 2 3 4 5
○ ○ ○ ○ ○
6 7 8 9 10

**H.** A lens that at its maximum aperture permits a relatively small amount of light to enter and pass through.

H
○ ○ ○ ○ ○
1 2 3 4 5
○ ○ ○ ○ ○
6 7 8 9 10

**I.** The extent of a scene that is visible through a particular lens.

I
○ ○ ○ ○ ○
1 2 3 4 5
○ ○ ○ ○ ○
6 7 8 9 10

**J.** Adjustable lens opening that controls the amount of light passing through the lens.

J
○ ○ ○ ○ ○
1 2 3 4 5
○ ○ ○ ○ ○
6 7 8 9 10

PAGE
TOTAL

SECTION
TOTAL

## REVIEW OF OPTICAL
## CHARACTERISTICS OF LENSES

*Select the correct answers and fill in the bubbles with the corresponding numbers.*

1. Assuming maximum aperture, a fast lens (11) *transmits an image faster* (12) *transmits and image more slowly* (13) *permits more light to enter* (14) *permits less light to enter.*

   **1** ○ ○ ○ ○
      11 12 13 14

2. Assuming maximum aperture, a slow lens (15) *transmits an image faster* (16) *transmits and image more slowly* (17) *permits more light to enter* (18) *permits less light to enter.*

   **2** ○ ○ ○ ○
      15 16 17 18

3. In the diagram below, select the most appropriate *f*-stop number for each of the four apertures (a through d) and fill in the bubbles with the corresponding number.

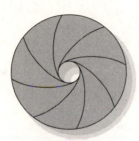

**a.** (19) *f*/1.4  (20) *f*/5.6  (21) *f*/22

**3a** ○    ○    ○
    19   20   21

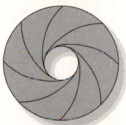

**b.** (22) *f*/1.4  (23) *f*/2.8  (24) *f*/16

**3b** ○    ○    ○
    22   23   24

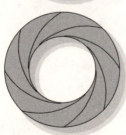

**c.** (25) *f*/1.4  (26) *f*/4  (27) *f*/16

**3c** ○    ○    ○
    25   26   27

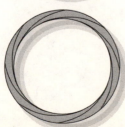

**d.** (28) *f*/1.4  (29) *f*/8  (30) *f*/22

**3d** ○    ○    ○
    28   29   30

PAGE
TOTAL [ ]

**4.** Telephoto lenses, or zoom lenses in a narrow-angle position, have a relatively (31) *shallow* (32) *narrow* (33) *great* depth of field.

**5.** The area in which all objects, although located at different distances from the camera, are in focus is called (34) *depth of focus* (35) *field of view* (36) *depth of field*.

**6.** Given a fixed camera-to-object distance, short-focal-length lenses, or zoom lenses in the wide-angle position, have a relatively (37) *shallow* (38) *wide* (39) *great* depth of field.

**7.** A 15x zoom lens means that you can increase the focal length (40) *1.5 times* (41) *15 times* (42) *150 times* in one continuous zoom.

**8.** Large apertures (iris openings) contribute to a (43) *great* (44) *shallow* depth of field.

**9.** When presetting (calibrating) the zoom lens, you (45) *zoom in all the way, focus on the target object, and zoom back* (46) *zoom out all the way to a long shot, focus on the target object, and zoom back in again.*

**10.** Select the three variables that influence depth of field: (47) *focal length of lens* (48) *zoom speed* (49) *focus* (50) *camera-to-object distance* (51) *lens aperture* (52) *focus mechanism.* **(Fill in three bubbles.)**

| **4** | ○ 31 | ○ 32 | ○ 33 |
|---|---|---|---|
| **5** | ○ 34 | ○ 35 | ○ 36 |
| **6** | ○ 37 | ○ 38 | ○ 39 |
| **7** | ○ 40 | ○ 41 | ○ 42 |
| **8** | ○ 43 | ○ 44 | |
| **9** | ○ 45 | ○ 46 | |
| **10** | ○ 47 | ○ 48 | ○ 49 |
| | ○ 50 | ○ 51 | ○ 52 |

P A G E
T O T A L

SECTION
TOTAL

## REVIEW OF DEPTH OF FIELD AND LENS ANGLES

*Select the correct answers and fill in the bubbles with the corresponding numbers.*

1.  A wide-angle lens (53) *increases* (54) *decreases* the illusion of depth and (55) *increases* (56) *decreases* the speed of an object moving toward or away from the camera. *(Fill in two bubbles.)*

    **1**  ◯ 53   ◯ 54
           ◯ 55   ◯ 56

2.  A narrow-angle lens makes objects positioned at different distances from the camera look (57) *more* (58) *less* crowded than they really are and (59) *increases* (60) *decreases* the speed of an object moving toward or away from the camera. *(Fill in two bubbles.)*

    **2**  ◯ 57   ◯ 58
           ◯ 59   ◯ 60

3.  To apply selective focus, we need (61) *a great* (62) *a shallow* depth of field.

    **3**  ◯ 61   ◯ 62

4.  To make a small room look larger, we use (63) *a wide-angle* (64) *a narrow-angle* lens.

    **4**  ◯ 63   ◯ 64

5.  The figure below shows the camera zoomed in all the way for a telephoto view and focused on object A. Object B will probably be (65) *in focus* (66) *out of focus*. The depth of field is therefore (67) *great* (68) *shallow*. *(Fill in two bubbles.)*

    **5**  ◯ 65   ◯ 66
           ◯ 67   ◯ 68

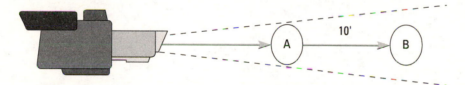

6.  The figure below shows the camera zoomed out all the way for a wide-angle view and focused on object A. Object B will probably be (69) *in focus* (70) *out of focus*. The depth of field is therefore (71) *great* (72) *shallow*. *(Fill in two bubbles.)*

    **6**  ◯ 69   ◯ 70
           ◯ 71   ◯ 72

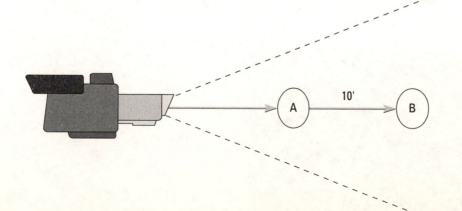

PAGE TOTAL [        ]

**7.** The screen image below displays (73) *a great* (74) *a shallow* depth of field.

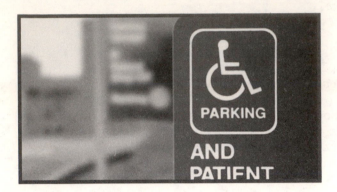

**8.** The screen image below shows that the camera's zoom lens was in (75) *a wide-angle* (76) *a narrow-angle* position.

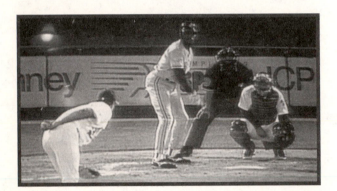

**9.** The opening shot of a documentary on city politics shows the city hall through a piece of sculpture. The camera operator used (77) *a wide-angle* (78) *a narrow-angle* position.

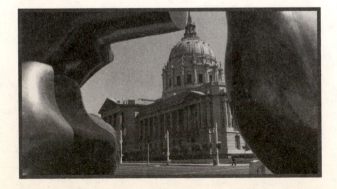

PAGE
TOTAL

*Chapter 4 — Lenses*

Course No. _____ Date _____ Name _____

**10.** Your preview monitors for cameras 1, 2, and 3 display the following images. Assuming that all three cameras are positioned right next to one another, which is the approximate zoom position for each? Choose among (79) *wide angle* (80) *normal* and (81) *narrow angle.*

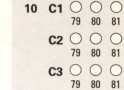

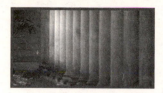

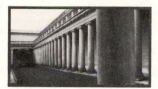

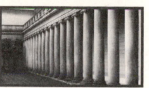

Camera 1                Camera 2                Camera 3

**11.** The figure below simulates (82) *an optical zoom* (83) *a digital zoom.*

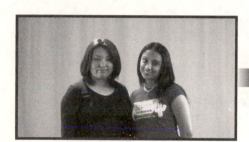

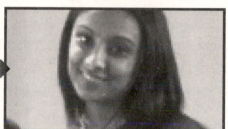

© 2006 Thomson Wadsworth

## REVIEW QUIZ

*Mark the following statements as true or false by filling in the bubbles in the* **T** *(for true) or* **F** *(for false) column.*

|   |   | T | F |
|---|---|---|---|
| **1.** | Digital stabilizers can absorb all picture wobble when you are shooting a narrow-angle picture. | **1** ○ 84 | ○ 85 |
| **2.** | After the initial calibration of a zoom lens, you need to preset it again each time the distance from object to camera changes substantially. | **2** ○ 86 | ○ 87 |
| **3.** | Depth of field is influenced only by the focal length of the lens. | **3** ○ 88 | ○ 89 |
| **4.** | You can use a neutral density filter to lower extreme brightness. | **4** ○ 90 | ○ 91 |
| **5.** | A slow lens is one with a very low *f*-stop number, such as *f*/1.4. | **5** ○ 92 | ○ 93 |
| **6.** | When covering a news story with an ENG/EFP camera, you are best off with a shallow depth of field because there are few, if any, focusing problems. | **6** ○ 94 | ○ 95 |
| **7.** | An object moving toward the camera looks faster than normal when shot with a wide-angle lens. | **7** ○ 96 | ○ 97 |
| **8.** | Because a 1080i HDTV image has so many scanning lines, the lens quality is relatively unimportant. | **8** ○ 98 | ○ 99 |
| **9.** | A zoom can be simulated by gradually enlarging the image's center portion. | **9** ○ 100 | ○ 101 |
| **10.** | We can dolly most easily when the lens is in the extreme wide-angle position. | **10** ○ 102 | ○ 103 |

SECTION
TOTAL [   ]

## ■ PROBLEM-SOLVING APPLICATIONS

*Let us now put the theory to work. You can observe the optical and performance characteristics of lenses easily by using a camcorder or a 35mm still camera that can accept various lenses. Think through each production problem and consider the various options, then pick the most effective solution and justify your choice.*

1. Zoom all the way out with the camcorder, or attach a wide-angle lens (28mm or less focal length) to the 35mm still camera, and focus on an object 4 to 6 feet away from you. Look at the background objects (20 or so feet away from you). Are they visible? Do they appear in fairly sharp focus? Or are they blurred? Now do the same observations by zooming all the way in or by attaching a telephoto lens (with a focal length of 200mm) to the still camera. Explain your observations with depth-of-field characteristics.

2. When watching television or a movie, try to figure out what lenses were used for some of the shots. For example, when you see someone running toward the camera yet seemingly not getting closer, what lens was used? Or when you see the happy couple approach the dinner table through the flowers and the candles in the foreground, what lens was probably used, assuming that the couple, as well as the candles and the flowers, are in focus? Such observations will certainly help you become more aware of focal lengths and their effects.

3. You are the AD of a live telecast of a modern dance program, which is performed on a dimly lighted stage. The operators of the two key cameras express some concern about their lenses. The new lens of the handheld ENG/EFP camera 1 has a 25× zoom range and a maximum aperture of ƒ/5.6. Although the lens was used successfully during the past three football games, the operator feels that it might be too slow for this type of application. Camera 2 has a 10× lens with a 2× range extender. Its maximum aperture is also ƒ/5.6. Are the operators' concerns justified?

4. The novice director asks you, the operator of camera 3, to get the opening shot by zooming back slowly from an extreme close-up of the title of a book to an extreme wide shot that shows a large part of the studio (the other cameras, the floor manager, the overhead lighting) as the background for the opening titles. The director sets up the wide shot first to make sure that it shows enough of the studio. When your extreme-narrow-angle zoom lens position does not produce the desired close-up of the title, he asks you to "simply pop in a range extender before we punch up your camera." What are the potential problems, if any? Be specific.

5. While shooting a dramatic program in the studio, the director notices that in your camera shot the focus on the background walls is very sharp. The director asks you to compose the shot so that the walls have a soft focus on them. What would you do?

# 5 Camera Mounting Equipment

## REVIEW OF KEY TERMS

*Match each term with its appropriate definition by filling in the corresponding bubble.*

1. cant
2. arc
3. dolly
4. camera pedestal

5. truck
6. Steadicam
7. fluid head

8. tilt
9. quick-release plate
10. pan

**A.** To move the camera laterally by means of a mobile camera mount.

A  ○ ○ ○ ○ ○
   1  2  3  4  5
  ○ ○ ○ ○ ○
   6  7  8  9  10

**B.** To move the camera in a slightly curved dolly or truck.

B  ○ ○ ○ ○ ○
   1  2  3  4  5
  ○ ○ ○ ○ ○
   6  7  8  9  10

**C.** Camera mount that helps produce jitter-free pictures even when the camera operator runs with it.

C  ○ ○ ○ ○ ○
   1  2  3  4  5
  ○ ○ ○ ○ ○
   6  7  8  9  10

**D.** To tilt a handheld camera sideways.

D  ○ ○ ○ ○ ○
   1  2  3  4  5
  ○ ○ ○ ○ ○
   6  7  8  9  10

**E.** To point the camera up or down.

E  ○ ○ ○ ○ ○
   1  2  3  4  5
  ○ ○ ○ ○ ○
   6  7  8  9  10

PAGE TOTAL ☐

| 1. cant | 5. truck | 8. tilt |
|---------|----------|---------|
| 2. arc | 6. Steadicam | 9. quick-release plate |
| 3. dolly | 7. fluid head | 10. pan |
| 4. camera pedestal | | |

**F.** To move the camera toward or away from an object.

F
○ ○ ○ ○ ○
1  2  3  4  5
○ ○ ○ ○ ○
6  7  8  9  10

**G.** Popular mounting head for lightweight ENG/EFP cameras.

G
○ ○ ○ ○ ○
1  2  3  4  5
○ ○ ○ ○ ○
6  7  8  9  10

**H.** Heavy camera dolly that can elevate and lower the camera while on the air.

H
○ ○ ○ ○ ○
1  2  3  4  5
○ ○ ○ ○ ○
6  7  8  9  10

**I.** Horizontal turning of the camera.

I
○ ○ ○ ○ ○
1  2  3  4  5
○ ○ ○ ○ ○
6  7  8  9  10

**J.** Device to attach an ENG/EFP camera to the fluid head.

J
○ ○ ○ ○ ○
1  2  3  4  5
○ ○ ○ ○ ○
6  7  8  9  10

PAGE TOTAL [        ]

SECTION TOTAL [        ]

## REVIEW OF CAMERA MOUNTS

*Select the correct answers and fill in the bubbles with the corresponding numbers.*

**1.** The spreader (11) *helps spread the tripod legs as much as possible* (12) *minimizes the spread of the tripod legs* (13) *keeps the tripod legs from spreading too far.*

**2.** The (14) *jib arm* (15) *monopod* (16) *leveling bowl* helps balance a camera on a pole.

**3.** Fluid and cam heads fulfill similar functions, but (17) *the fluid head* (18) *the cam head* is designed to handle the heavier studio cameras.

**4.** A (19) *wedge mount* (20) *robotic pedestal* (21) *quick-release plate* makes it possible to quickly attach/detach an ENG/EFP camera from the tripod.

**5.** For all normal camera moves, the pedestal is usually set for (22) *tricycle* (23) *parallel* (24) *independent* steering.

| | | | |
|---|---|---|---|
| **1** | ○ 11 | ○ 12 | ○ 13 |
| **2** | ○ 14 | ○ 15 | ○ 16 |
| **3** | ○ 17 | ○ 18 | |
| **4** | ○ 19 | ○ 20 | ○ 21 |
| **5** | ○ 22 | ○ 23 | ○ 24 |

PAGE TOTAL ☐

© 2006 Thomson Wadsworth

**6.** Fill in the bubbles whose numbers correspond with the camera movements indicated in the following figure.

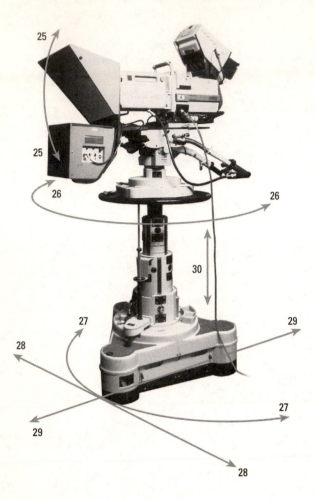

**a.** dolly

**b.** truck

**c.** tilt

**d.** pan

**e.** pedestal

**f.** arc

6a  ○25  ○26  ○27
    ○28  ○29  ○30

6b  ○25  ○26  ○27
    ○28  ○29  ○30

6c  ○25  ○26  ○27
    ○28  ○29  ○30

6d  ○25  ○26  ○27
    ○28  ○29  ○30

6e  ○25  ○26  ○27
    ○28  ○29  ○30

6f  ○25  ○26  ○27
    ○28  ○29  ○30

PAGE TOTAL

SECTION TOTAL

## REVIEW QUIZ

*Mark the following statements as true or false by filling in the bubbles in the* **T** *(for true) and* **F** *(for false) column.*

|   |   | T | F |
|---|---|---|---|
| **1.** | The drag controls on a camera mounting head are used to lock down the camera. | **1** ○ 31 | ○ 32 |
| **2.** | Because an ENG camera can be shoulder-mounted, the operator has no need for a tripod. | **2** ○ 33 | ○ 34 |
| **3.** | A robotic pedestal is motor-driven. | **3** ○ 35 | ○ 36 |
| **4.** | Although we can tilt smoothly with a cam head, we cannot do so with a fluid head. | **4** ○ 37 | ○ 38 |
| **5.** | The wedge mount ensures that the camera is mounted in an optimally balanced position. | **5** ○ 39 | ○ 40 |
| **6.** | Dolly and truck movements show up as similar movements on the screen. | **6** ○ 41 | ○ 42 |
| **7.** | To boom up means to raise the camera pedestal. | **7** ○ 43 | ○ 44 |
| **8.** | The studio pedestal permits very low angle shots. | **8** ○ 45 | ○ 46 |
| **9.** | The jib arm and the camera crane can make the camera move in similar ways. | **9** ○ 47 | ○ 48 |
| **10.** | Tilting a shoulder-mounted camera sideways is called panning. | **10** ○ 49 | ○ 50 |

**SECTION TOTAL** [     ]

1. Locate the pan and the tilt drag controls and the pan-and-tilt lock controls of the camera. Adjust them so that you can pan and tilt the camera as smoothly as necessary. When do you need to use the lock mechanism?

2. Pedestal up and down to see how high and low the camera will go. What can happen if you move the camera too fast to either end of vertical travel?

3. Your director asks you, the EFP camera operator, to attach a heavy teleprompter to your EFP camcorder, which is mounted on a normal field tripod with a fluid head. What is your response?

4. You are to set up a tripod on an uneven, slightly sloping field. How can you make sure that the tripod and, with it, the EFP camera are level?

5. The director wants you to follow the new mayor up the flight of stairs in city hall without shaking the ENG/EFP camera. What camera mount would you suggest?

6. You are shooting a documentary-style program, and you don't have a tripod at the shoot. What focal length would be most effective if you want relatively steady shots? What other techniques could you consider for getting steady shots?

7. You have been asked to recommend the types of camera mounting equipment for a four-camera studio production. The director wants one camera to get a moving overhead shot and another camera that can physically move around the floor in a smooth arcing motion. The other two cameras will be shooting a variety of typical long shots and close-ups. Another consideration is that there will be only three camera operators available during the production. List the types of mounting equipment you would recommend for each camera and why.

# 6 Camera Operation and Picture Composition

## REVIEW OF KEY TERMS

*Match each term with its appropriate definition by filling in the corresponding bubble.*

1. close-up
2. closure
3. cross-shot
4. follow focus

5. headroom
6. noseroom
7. AGC

8. leadroom
9. over-the-shoulder shot
10. shot sheet

**A.** An automatic audio volume control.

A  ○ ○ ○ ○ ○
   1  2  3  4  5
   ○ ○ ○ ○ ○
   6  7  8  9  10

**B.** Maintaining focus as the camera and/or object moves.

B  ○ ○ ○ ○ ○
   1  2  3  4  5
   ○ ○ ○ ○ ○
   6  7  8  9  10

**C.** The space left in front of a person facing and moving toward the edge of the screen.

C  ○ ○ ○ ○ ○
   1  2  3  4  5
   ○ ○ ○ ○ ○
   6  7  8  9  10

**D.** Similar to the over-the-shoulder shot except that the camera-near person is completely out of the shot.

D  ○ ○ ○ ○ ○
   1  2  3  4  5
   ○ ○ ○ ○ ○
   6  7  8  9  10

**E.** The space left between the top of the head and the upper screen edge.

E  ○ ○ ○ ○ ○
   1  2  3  4  5
   ○ ○ ○ ○ ○
   6  7  8  9  10

PAGE TOTAL ☐

| | | |
|---|---|---|
| 1. close-up | 5. headroom | 8. leadroom |
| 2. closure | 6. noseroom | 9. over-the-shoulder shot |
| 3. cross-shot | 7. AGC | 10. shot sheet |
| 4. follow focus | | |

**F.** Object or any part of it seen at close range.

F   ○ ○ ○ ○ ○
    1   2   3   4   5
    ○ ○ ○ ○ ○
    6   7   8   9   10

**G.** The space left in front of a person looking toward the screen edge.

G   ○ ○ ○ ○ ○
    1   2   3   4   5
    ○ ○ ○ ○ ○
    6   7   8   9   10

**H.** A handwritten card that lists each take for a camera.

H   ○ ○ ○ ○ ○
    1   2   3   4   5
    ○ ○ ○ ○ ○
    6   7   8   9   10

**I.** Mentally filling in spaces of an incomplete picture.

I   ○ ○ ○ ○ ○
    1   2   3   4   5
    ○ ○ ○ ○ ○
    6   7   8   9   10

**J.** Camera looks at the camera-far person with the back and shoulder of the camera-near person in the shot.

J   ○ ○ ○ ○ ○
    1   2   3   4   5
    ○ ○ ○ ○ ○
    6   7   8   9   10

PAGE TOTAL [ ]

SECTION TOTAL [ ]

## REVIEW OF HOW TO WORK A CAMERA

*Select the correct answers and fill in the bubbles with the corresponding numbers.*

**1.** After having calibrated the zoom lens, you need to preset it again  (11) *only when the camera moves*  (12) *only when the object moves relative to the camera*  (13) *whenever camera or object moves relative to the other.*

**1**  ◯ 11   ◯ 12   ◯ 13

**2.** When dollying with a studio camera, or walking with an EFP camera, the zoom lens should be in  (14) *a narrow-angle position*  (15) *a telephoto position*  (16) *a wide-angle position.*

**2**  ◯ 14   ◯ 15   ◯ 16

**3.** When dollying with a studio camera, or walking with an EFP camera, the depth of field should be as  (17) *great*  (18) *shallow*  (19) *narrow* as possible.

**3**  ◯ 17   ◯ 18   ◯ 19

**4.** When panning with a shoulder-mounted ENG/EFP camera, you should point your knees toward  (20) *the starting point of the pan*  (21) *the end point of the pan*  (22) *either direction.*

**4**  ◯ 20   ◯ 21   ◯ 22

**5.** During a test recording with your ENG/EFP camcorder, you should  (23) *leave the lens cap on but check the audio*  (24) *make sure all camera features are working*  (25) *ask the reporter to count to ten.*

**5**  ◯ 23   ◯ 24   ◯ 25

**6.** BNC and RCA phono plugs  (26) *can be connected without any problem because they are basically the same*  (27) *can be connected with an adapter*  (28) *are totally incompatible.*

**6**  ◯ 26   ◯ 27   ◯ 28

**7.** To calibrate a zoom lens  (29) *zoom in, focus, zoom out to shot*  (30) *zoom out, focus, zoom in to shot*  (31) *adjust focus continuously while zooming.*

**7**  ◯ 29   ◯ 30   ◯ 31

**8.** You should lock the camera mounting head  (32) *every time you leave it*  (33) *only when temporarily leaving the camera*  (34) *at the end of the shoot.*

**8**  ◯ 32   ◯ 33   ◯ 34

**9.** When loading a VTR cassette for recording, the safety tab  (35) *should be in place or in the closed position*  (36) *should be removed or in the open position*  (37) *does not matter because it is primarily meant for playback protection.*

**9**  ◯ 35   ◯ 36   ◯ 37

**10.** When on an ENG assignment, you should record ambient sound  (38) *only if somebody is talking*  (39) *always*  (40) *only if there is no background noise.*

**10**  ◯ 38   ◯ 39   ◯ 40

SECTION TOTAL [　　]

## REVIEW OF FRAMING A SHOT AND PICTURE COMPOSITION

1. Using the set of numbered images below, fill in the bubbles for each of the following fields of view or shot designations.

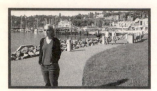
41

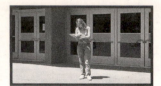
42

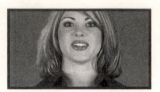
43

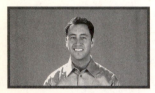
44

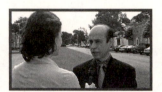
45

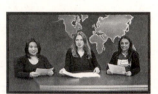
46

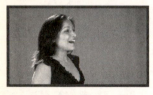
47

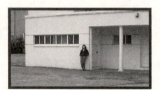
48

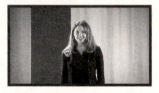
49

**a.** ELS (extreme long shot)

1a ◯ ◯ ◯ ◯ ◯
   41 42 43 44 45
   ◯ ◯ ◯ ◯
   46 47 48 49

**b.** LS (long shot)

1b ◯ ◯ ◯ ◯ ◯
   41 42 43 44 45
   ◯ ◯ ◯ ◯
   46 47 48 49

PAGE
TOTAL

**c.** MS (medium shot)

**d.** CU (close-up)

**1d** ○ ○ ○ ○ ○
41 42 43 44 45
○ ○ ○ ○
46 47 48 49

**e.** ECU (extreme close-up)

**1e** ○ ○ ○ ○ ○
41 42 43 44 45
○ ○ ○ ○
46 47 48 49

**f.** three-shot

**1f** ○ ○ ○ ○ ○
41 42 43 44 45
○ ○ ○ ○
46 47 48 49

**g.** knee shot

**1g** ○ ○ ○ ○ ○
41 42 43 44 45
○ ○ ○ ○
46 47 48 49

**h.** bust shot

**1h** ○ ○ ○ ○ ○
41 42 43 44 45
○ ○ ○ ○
46 47 48 49

**i.** over-the-shoulder shot

**1i** ○ ○ ○ ○ ○
41 42 43 44 45
○ ○ ○ ○
46 47 48 49

PAGE
TOTAL _____

**2.** Evaluate the framing of shots in the next five figures by filling in the bubbles with the corresponding numbers. *(Note: There may be more than one correct answer for some parts of a problem.)*

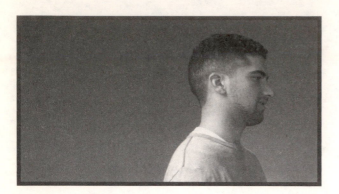

**a.** This shot is (50) *acceptable* (51) *unacceptable* because it has (52) *sufficient noseroom* (53) *insufficient noseroom* (54) *sufficient headroom* (55) *insufficient leadroom.* If unacceptable, you should (56) *pan left* (57) *pan right* (58) *tilt up* (59) *tilt down* (60) *pedestal up* (61) *pedestal down.*

**2a** ○ ○
    50   51

○ ○ ○ ○
52 53 54 55

○ ○ ○
56 57 58

○ ○ ○
59 60 61

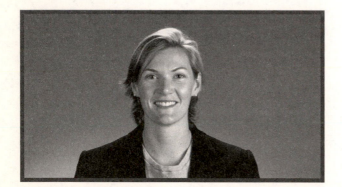

**b.** This CU is (62) *acceptable* (63) *unacceptable* because it has (64) *no headroom* (65) *too much headroom* (66) *adequate headroom* (67) *adequate noseroom.* If unacceptable, you should (68) *tilt up* (69) *tilt down* (70) *pan left.*

**2b** ○ ○
    62   63

○ ○ ○ ○
64 65 66 67

○ ○ ○
68 69 70

PAGE
TOTAL

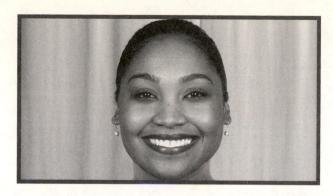

c. This shot is (71) *acceptable* (72) *unacceptable* because it has (73) *no headroom* (74) *too much headroom* (75) *no noseroom* (76) *no leadroom* (77) *insufficient clues for closure in off-screen space*. If unacceptable, you should (78) *tilt up* (79) *tilt down*.

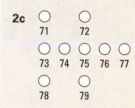

2c  ○ ○
    71  72
    ○ ○ ○ ○ ○
    73 74 75 76 77
    ○ ○
    78  79

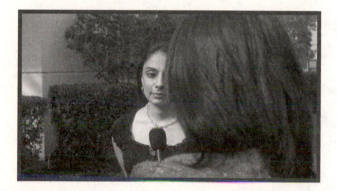

d. This over-the-shoulder shot is (80) *acceptable* (81) *unacceptable*. If unacceptable, you should (82) *zoom out* (83) *pedestal up* (84) *arc left* (85) *arc right*.

2d  ○ ○
    80  81
    ○ ○ ○ ○
    82 83 84 85

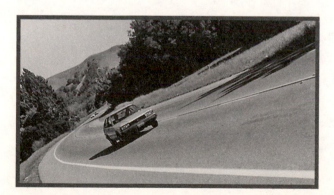

e. This shot is intended to emphasize the car's speed and risky driving. Its framing is, therefore, (86) *acceptable* (87) *unacceptable*. If unacceptable, you should (88) *level the horizon line* (89) *zoom out*.

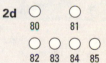

2e  ○ ○
    86  87
    ○ ○
    88  89

P A G E
T O T A L  [        ]

**3.** This framimg is  (90) *acceptable*  (91) *unacceptable* in terms of closure.

3 ○ ○
    90  91

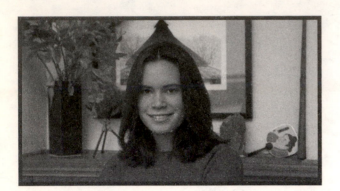

**4.** This shot makes  (92) *good*  (93) *poor*  use of screen depth. If depth improvement is needed, you should  (94) *add*  (95) *delete* foreground objects.

4 ○ ○
    92  93
    ○ ○
    94  95

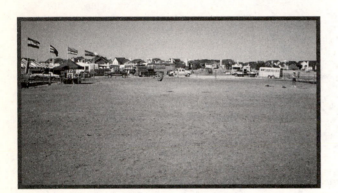

PAGE
TOTAL

SECTION
TOTAL

# REVIEW QUIZ

*Mark the following statements as true or false by filling in the bubbles in the*
***T*** *(for true) or **F** (for false) column.*

|  | T | F |
|---|---|---|

1. Before the studio or remote production, you should check the tightest and widest field of view of your zoom lens from the principal camera position.  **1** ○ 96  ○ 97

2. You should unlock the pan-and-tilt mechanism at the beginning of the show and lock it again every time you leave the camera unattended.  **2** ○ 98  ○ 99

3. Because some camcorders have a shoulder mount, there is no need for a tripod.  **3** ○ 100  ○ 101

4. If your camcorder has an LCD panel, you should use it to focus whenever possible.  **4** ○ 102  ○ 103

5. HDTV cameras are easier to focus than standard cameras.  **5** ○ 104  ○ 105

6. When operating an ENG/EFP camera, walking backward will make it easier to keep the camera steady than walking forward.  **6** ○ 106  ○ 107

7. Leadroom and noseroom fulfill similar framing (compositional) functions.  **7** ○ 108  ○ 109

8. Field of view refers to how far or close the object appears relative to the camera.  **8** ○ 110  ○ 111

9. Psychological closure always ensures good composition.  **9** ○ 112  ○ 113

10. Zooming all the way out will help minimize camera wobbles.  **10** ○ 114  ○ 115

11. Motion toward or away from the camera is on the z-axis  **11** ○ 116  ○ 117

SECTION TOTAL [ ]

## PROBLEM-SOLVING APPLICATIONS

1. During the remote coverage of the World Computer Fair, the novice director tells you to zoom in to an ECU of a computer display, then arc the tripod dolly around the display table to show the other computers. What are the potential problems, if any?

2. In a multicamera studio dance program, the same director tells you, the operator of camera 3, that you should listen only to calls that concern your camera and ignore commands to all the other cameras. Do you agree? If so, why? If not, why not?

3. As you are leaving the studio, the producer states that a spare battery for your ENG/EFP camera is not needed because the story you are to cover will have, at best, a 20-second slot in the newscast. What is your response?

4. The producer tells you to be sure to keep enough headroom when framing an ECU. Do you agree? Why? If not, why not?

5. The director tells you, the camera operator, to change from an over-the-shoulder shot to a cross-shot. How can you accomplish such a shot change?

6. You are on location, setting up your tripod and camera. As you look in the viewfinder to frame your first shot, you notice that the horizon line is tilted. The tripod cannot be moved to a different spot. How can you level the camera?

# 7 Lighting

## REVIEW OF KEY TERMS

*Match each term with its appropriate definition by filling in the corresponding bubble.*

1. **barn doors**
2. **baselight**
3. **spotlight**
4. **reflected light**
5. **incident light**
6. **dimmer**
7. **foot-candle**
8. **floodlight**
9. **cucoloris**

**A.** Even, nondirectional (diffused) light necessary for the camera to operate optimally.

A ○ ○ ○ ○ ○
  1 2 3 4 5
  ○ ○ ○ ○
  6 7 8 9

**B.** Metal flaps in front of lighting instruments that control the spread of the light beam.

B ○ ○ ○ ○ ○
  1 2 3 4 5
  ○ ○ ○ ○
  6 7 8 9

**C.** A lighting instrument that produces directional, relatively undiffused light.

C ○ ○ ○ ○ ○
  1 2 3 4 5
  ○ ○ ○ ○
  6 7 8 9

**D.** A lighting instrument that produces diffused light with a relatively undefined beam edge.

D ○ ○ ○ ○ ○
  1 2 3 4 5
  ○ ○ ○ ○
  6 7 8 9

**E.** Light that is bounced off the illuminated object.

E ○ ○ ○ ○ ○
  1 2 3 4 5
  ○ ○ ○ ○
  6 7 8 9

PAGE TOTAL ☐

© 2006 Thomson Wadsworth

| 1. barn doors | 4. reflected light | 7. foot-candle |
|---|---|---|
| 2. baselight | 5. incident light | 8. floodlight |
| 3. spotlight | 6. dimmer | 9. cucoloris |

**F.** The American unit of measurement of illumination, or the amount of light that falls on an object.

F ○ ○ ○ ○ ○
  1 2 3 4 5
  ○ ○ ○ ○
  6 7 8 9

**G.** Light that strikes the object directly from its source.

G ○ ○ ○ ○ ○
  1 2 3 4 5
  ○ ○ ○ ○
  6 7 8 9

**H.** A metal cutout for a pattern projection.

H ○ ○ ○ ○ ○
  1 2 3 4 5
  ○ ○ ○ ○
  6 7 8 9

**I.** A device that controls light intensity.

I ○ ○ ○ ○ ○
  1 2 3 4 5
  ○ ○ ○ ○
  6 7 8 9

PAGE TOTAL

SECTION TOTAL

## REVIEW OF LIGHTING INSTRUMENTS AND CONTROLS

1. One foot-candle is approximately (10) *1* (11) *10* (12) *100* lux.

2. When measuring baselight, you need to read (13) *incident* (14) *reflected* (15) *directional* light.

3. When measuring incident light, you point the foot-candle or lux meter (16) *toward the set* (17) *toward the camera lens* (18) *close to the lighted object.*

4. When reading reflected light, you point the light meter (19) *close to the lighted object* (20) *into the lights* (21) *toward the camera lens.*

5. The beam of softlights (22) *cannot be adjusted* (23) *can be adjusted by a focus control* (24) *can be adjusted by moving the lamp assembly toward or away from the reflector.*

6. To flood (spread) the light beam of a Fresnel spotlight, you need to move the lamp-reflector unit (25) *toward* (26) *away from* the lens.

7. With the use of the patchboard (or computer patching), you can link (27) *only one instrument* (28) *several instruments* (29) *all available instruments simultaneously* to a specific dimmer.

| | | | |
|---|---|---|---|
| 1 | ○ 10 | ○ 11 | ○ 12 |
| 2 | ○ 13 | ○ 14 | ○ 15 |
| 3 | ○ 16 | ○ 17 | ○ 18 |
| 4 | ○ 19 | ○ 20 | ○ 21 |
| 5 | ○ 22 | ○ 23 | ○ 24 |
| 6 | ○ 25 | ○ 26 | |
| 7 | ○ 27 | ○ 28 | ○ 29 |

PAGE TOTAL [____]

**8.** Fill in the bubbles whose numbers correspond with the appropriate lighting instruments shown below.

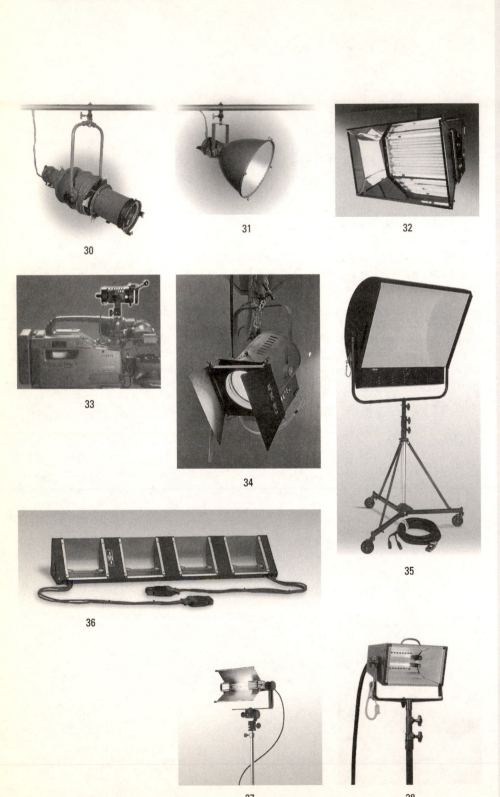

30

31

32

33

34

35

36

37

38

**a.** V-light

8a  ○ ○ ○ ○ ○
    30 31 32 33 34
    ○ ○ ○ ○
    35 36 37 38

**b.** strip, or cyc, light

8b  ○ ○ ○ ○ ○
    30 31 32 33 34
    ○ ○ ○ ○
    35 36 37 38

**c.** fluorescent floodlight bank

8c  ○ ○ ○ ○ ○
    30 31 32 33 34
    ○ ○ ○ ○
    35 36 37 38

**d.** Fresnel spotlight

8d  ○ ○ ○ ○ ○
    30 31 32 33 34
    ○ ○ ○ ○
    35 36 37 38

**e.** scoop

8e  ○ ○ ○ ○ ○
    30 31 32 33 34
    ○ ○ ○ ○
    35 36 37 38

**f.** ellipsoidal spotlight

8f  ○ ○ ○ ○ ○
    30 31 32 33 34
    ○ ○ ○ ○
    35 36 37 38

**g.** softlight

8g  ○ ○ ○ ○ ○
    30 31 32 33 34
    ○ ○ ○ ○
    35 36 37 38

**h.** camera light

8h  ○ ○ ○ ○ ○
    30 31 32 33 34
    ○ ○ ○ ○
    35 36 37 38

**i.** broad

8i  ○ ○ ○ ○ ○
    30 31 32 33 34
    ○ ○ ○ ○
    35 36 37 38

PAGE TOTAL [    ]

**9.** Fill in the bubbles whose numbers correspond with the numbers identifying the various parts of the spotlight shown below.

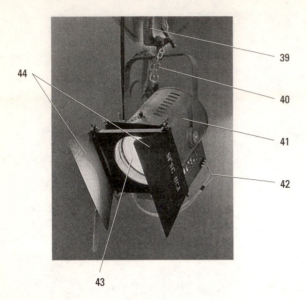

**a.** C-clamp

**b.** Fresnel lens

**c.** two-way barn doors

**d.** safety chain

**e.** power cord

**f.** lamp housing

**10.** A dimmer controls (45) *the wattage of the lamp* (46) *the flow of voltage to the lamp* (47) *the amperes flowing to the lamp.*

**9a** ○ 39  ○ 40  ○ 41
○ 42  ○ 43  ○ 44

**9b** ○ 39  ○ 40  ○ 41
○ 42  ○ 43  ○ 44

**9c** ○ 39  ○ 40  ○ 41
○ 42  ○ 43  ○ 44

**9d** ○ 39  ○ 40  ○ 41
○ 42  ○ 43  ○ 44

**9e** ○ 39  ○ 40  ○ 41
○ 42  ○ 43  ○ 44

**9f** ○ 39  ○ 40  ○ 41
○ 42  ○ 43  ○ 44

**10** ○ 45  ○ 46  ○ 47

PAGE TOTAL

SECTION TOTAL

## REVIEW QUIZ

*Mark the following statements as true or false by filling in the bubbles in the*
***T*** *(for true) or* ***F*** *(for false) column.*

|  | | T | F |
|---|---|---|---|
| **1.** | The optimal contrast ratio for most standard television cameras is 40:1 to 50:1. | **1** ○ 48 | ○ 49 |
| **2.** | To illuminate a large area with even light, we use a variety of Fresnel spots. | **2** ○ 50 | ○ 51 |
| **3.** | Barn doors are primarily used for intensity control. | **3** ○ 52 | ○ 53 |
| **4.** | Focusing a light results in sharper shadows. | **4** ○ 54 | ○ 55 |
| **5.** | Portable fluorescent banks are used to illuminate areas with even light. | **5** ○ 56 | ○ 57 |
| **6.** | When necessary, the beam of softlights can be focused. | **6** ○ 58 | ○ 59 |
| **7.** | The shutters on an ellipsoidal spot can shape its beam. | **7** ○ 60 | ○ 61 |
| **8.** | A flag has a similar function to barn doors. | **8** ○ 62 | ○ 63 |
| **9.** | Incident light can be measured by pointing the light meter into the lights or toward the camera lens. | **9** ○ 64 | ○ 65 |
| **10.** | Regardless of the type of dimmer control, all patching must be done with patch cords for each instrument. | **10** ○ 66 | ○ 67 |

SECTION TOTAL ▭

## PROBLEM-SOLVING APPLICATIONS

1. You are asked to raise the baselight level in a classroom for optimal camera performance. Even though the small portable spotlights are in the maximum flood position, the additional illumination is not even. What other methods do you have available to achieve further diffusion?

2. You are asked to produce extremely sharp beams that reflect as precise pools of light on the studio floor. What type of lighting instruments would you use?

3. When checking the general baselight level and the amount of foot-candles (or lux) falling on the subject, the lighting assistant first stands next to the lighted subject and points the light meter toward the principal camera position and then at the various lighting instruments illuminating the subject. Will the assistant's action produce the desired results? If so, why? If not, why not?

4. You are asked to assemble a lighting kit that will be useful for lighting indoor interviews in small rooms, such as hotel rooms or offices. What instruments and other necessary equipment would you recommend?

5. You are asked to dim all spotlights simultaneously and then do the same thing immediately thereafter with all floodlights. How can you best accomplish this task?

# 8 Techniques of Television Lighting

Course No. _____   Date _____   Name _____

## REVIEW OF KEY TERMS

*Match each term with its appropriate definition by filling in the corresponding bubble.*

1. silhouette
2. fill light
3. background light
4. back light
5. side light
6. kicker light
7. high key
8. low key
9. key light
10. color temperature
11. falloff
12. photographic lighting principle

**A.** Illumination from behind the subject and opposite the camera.

A: ○1 ○2 ○3 ○4 ○5 ○6 ○7 ○8 ○9 ○10 ○11 ○12

**B.** Dark background, with a few selective light sources on the scene.

B: ○1 ○2 ○3 ○4 ○5 ○6 ○7 ○8 ○9 ○10 ○11 ○12

**C.** Illumination of the set, set pieces, and backdrops.

C: ○1 ○2 ○3 ○4 ○5 ○6 ○7 ○8 ○9 ○10 ○11 ○12

**D.** The speed with which a light picture portion turns into shadow area.

D: ○1 ○2 ○3 ○4 ○5 ○6 ○7 ○8 ○9 ○10 ○11 ○12

PAGE TOTAL ☐

© 2006 Thomson Wadsworth

| 1. silhouette | 5. side light | 9. key light |
|---|---|---|
| 2. fill light | 6. kicker light | 10. color temperature |
| 3. background light | 7. high key | 11. falloff |
| 4. back light | 8. low key | 12. photographic lighting principle |

**E.** The triangular arrangement of the three major light sources used to illuminate a subject.

E   ○ ○ ○ ○
    1  2  3  4
    ○ ○ ○ ○
    5  6  7  8
    ○ ○ ○ ○
    9 10 11 12

**F.** Additional light that illuminates shadow areas and thereby reduces falloff.

F   ○ ○ ○ ○
    1  2  3  4
    ○ ○ ○ ○
    5  6  7  8
    ○ ○ ○ ○
    9 10 11 12

**G.** Unlighted subject in front of a brightly illuminated background.

G   ○ ○ ○ ○
    1  2  3  4
    ○ ○ ○ ○
    5  6  7  8
    ○ ○ ○ ○
    9 10 11 12

**H.** The relative reddishness or bluishness of white light.

H   ○ ○ ○ ○
    1  2  3  4
    ○ ○ ○ ○
    5  6  7  8
    ○ ○ ○ ○
    9 10 11 12

**I.** Light background and ample light on the scene.

I   ○ ○ ○ ○
    1  2  3  4
    ○ ○ ○ ○
    5  6  7  8
    ○ ○ ○ ○
    9 10 11 12

PAGE TOTAL [          ]

| | | |
|---|---|---|
| 1. silhouette | 5. side light | 9. key light |
| 2. fill light | 6. kicker light | 10. color temperature |
| 3. background light | 7. high key | 11. falloff |
| 4. back light | 8. low key | 12. photographic lighting principle |

**J.** Principal source of illumination.

J  ○ ○ ○ ○
   1  2  3  4
  ○ ○ ○ ○
   5  6  7  8
  ○ ○ ○ ○
   9 10 11 12

**K.** Directional light coming from the side and the back of the subject, usually from below.

K  ○ ○ ○ ○
   1  2  3  4
  ○ ○ ○ ○
   5  6  7  8
  ○ ○ ○ ○
   9 10 11 12

**L.** Directional light from the side of an object.

L  ○ ○ ○ ○
   1  2  3  4
  ○ ○ ○ ○
   5  6  7  8
  ○ ○ ○ ○
   9 10 11 12

PAGE TOTAL [ ]

SECTION TOTAL [ ]

## REVIEW OF LIGHTING TECHNIQUES

*Select the correct answers and fill in the bubbles with the corresponding numbers.*

1. The arrangement of the lighting instruments shown in the following figure is generally called (13) *four-point lighting* (14) *photographic lighting principle* (15) *field lighting principle.*

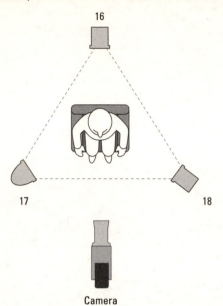

16

17          18

Camera

2. Fill in the bubbles whose numbers correspond with the functions of the lighting instruments shown in the figure above and whether they are usually (S) *spotlights* or (F) *floodlights.*

   **a.** key

   **b.** back

   **c.** fill

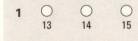

| 1 | ○ 13 | ○ 14 | ○ 15 |

| 2a | ○ 16 | ○ 17 | ○ 18 |
| | ○ S | ○ F | |

| 2b | ○ 16 | ○ 17 | ○ 18 |
| | ○ S | ○ F | |

| 2c | ○ 16 | ○ 17 | ○ 18 |
| | ○ S | ○ F | |

PAGE
TOTAL

**3.** What major light sources were used to illuminate the host of a sports show in the following four pictures? In the diagrams, circle the instrument(s) used, then fill in the bubbles whose numbers correspond with the instruments used to light the subject.

**a.**

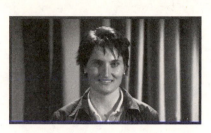

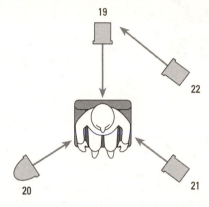

19
22
20
21

**3a** ◯ ◯ ◯ ◯
   19 20 21 22

**b.**

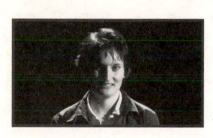

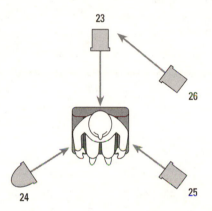

23
26
24
25

**3b** ◯ ◯ ◯ ◯
   23 24 25 26

**c.**

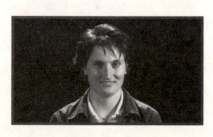

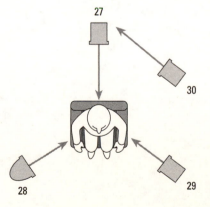

27
30
28
29

**3c** ◯ ◯ ◯ ◯
   27 28 29 30

PAGE
TOTAL [　　　]

**d.**

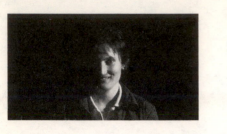

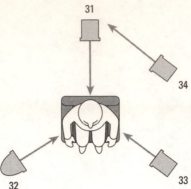

**4.** You are to evaluate normal lighting setups. In the following five figures, cross out the lighting instruments that are unnecessary or most likely to interfere with the intended lighting effects, then fill in the bubbles whose numbers correspond with the instruments *needed*.

**a.** Newscast

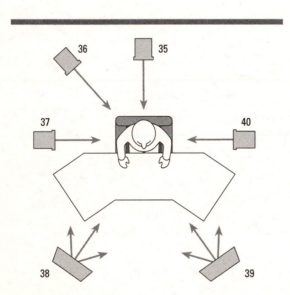

4a  ◯        ◯        ◯
   35       36       37
   ◯        ◯        ◯
   38       39       40

PAGE
TOTAL

**b.** Cameo lighting

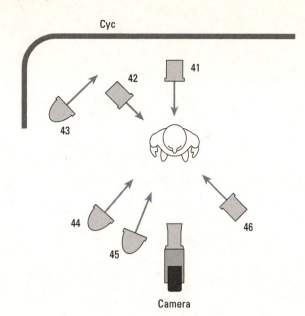

**c.** Dancer in silhouette

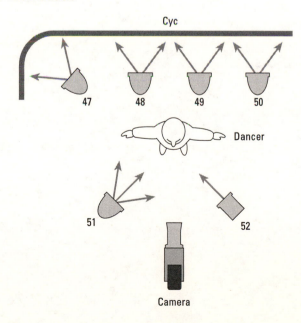

4b  ○ 41   ○ 42   ○ 43
    ○ 44   ○ 45   ○ 46

4c  ○ 47   ○ 48   ○ 49
    ○ 50   ○ 51   ○ 52

PAGE
TOTAL [ ]

*Chapter 8* — *Techniques of Television Lighting*

**d.** Speaker and audience

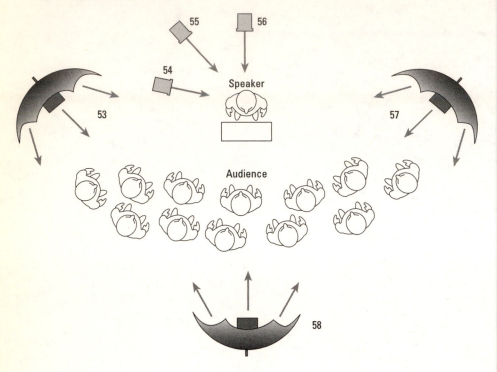

**e.** Chroma-key area lighting

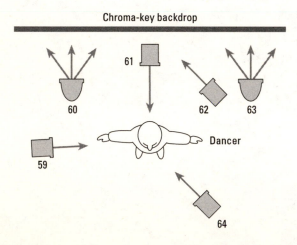

**4d**  ○ 53   ○ 54   ○ 55
        ○ 56   ○ 57   ○ 58

**4e**  ○ 59   ○ 60   ○ 61
        ○ 62   ○ 63   ○ 64

PAGE
TOTAL [        ]

5. When shooting an ENG interview in bright sunlight, the most convenient fill light is (65) *an HMI spot* (66) *a quartz scoop* (67) *a reflector.*

| 5 | ○ 65 | ○ 66 | ○ 67 |

6. The color temperature of a light can be raised by using (68) *an orange gel* (69) *a blue gel* (70) *an amber gel.*

| 6 | ○ 68 | ○ 69 | ○ 70 |

7. The usual power rating per circuit of ordinary household wall outlets is (71) *15 amps* (72) *50 amps* (73) *150 amps.*

| 7 | ○ 71 | ○ 72 | ○ 73 |

8. To figure the total wattage that a circuit can safely carry, you should multiply the number of amps by (74) *15* (75) *75* (76) *100.*

| 8 | ○ 74 | ○ 75 | ○ 76 |

9. Having somebody stand in front of a brightly illuminated building will (77) *provide much needed back light* (78) *help separate the person from the background* (79) *cause an undesirable silhouette effect.*

| 9 | ○ 77 | ○ 78 | ○ 79 |

10. Excessive dimming (more than 10 percent of full power) will (80) *increase* (81) *decrease* (82) *not affect* the color temperature. This means that the white light will (83) *remain basically unchanged* (84) *turn reddish* (85) *turn bluish.* **(Fill in two bubbles.)**

| 10 | ○ 80 | ○ 81 | ○ 82 |
|    | ○ 83 | ○ 84 | ○ 85 |

11. To make a model's hair look especially glamorous, you need a high-intensity (86) *key light* (87) *background light* (88) *back light.*

| 11 | ○ 86 | ○ 87 | ○ 88 |

12. To achieve fast falloff, you need to use primarily (89) *spotlights* (90) *floodlights* (91) *fluorescent lights.*

| 12 | ○ 89 | ○ 90 | ○ 91 |

13. The standard color temperature for outdoor light is (92) *3,200K* (93) *3,600K* (94) *5,600K.*

| 13 | ○ 92 | ○ 93 | ○ 94 |

14. To light the backdrop for a chroma key, you need (95) *ellipsoidal spotlights* (96) *Fresnel spotlights* (97) *floodlights.*

| 14 | ○ 95 | ○ 96 | ○ 97 |

PAGE TOTAL

SECTION TOTAL

*Mark the following statements as true or false by filling in the bubbles in the*
*T (for true) or F (for false) column.*

|   |   | T | F |
|---|---|---|---|
| **1.** | The photographic lighting principle, or triangle lighting, uses a key light, a kicker light, and a back light. | 1 ○ 98 | ○ 99 |
| **2.** | Back lights and background lights fulfill similar functions. | 2 ○ 100 | ○ 101 |
| **3.** | High-key lighting means that the key light strikes the subject from above eye level. | 3 ○ 102 | ○ 103 |
| **4.** | The background light must strike the background from the same side as the key light. | 4 ○ 104 | ○ 105 |
| **5.** | In multiple-function lighting, the key light can act as a back light, and the side light as key, depending on the position of the camera relative to the subject. | 5 ○ 106 | ○ 107 |
| **6.** | The more fill light, the slower the falloff. | 6 ○ 108 | ○ 109 |
| **7.** | Low-key lighting means that the lighting is soft and even, with extremely slow falloff. | 7 ○ 110 | ○ 111 |
| **8.** | All cameo lighting is highly directional. | 8 ○ 112 | ○ 113 |
| **9.** | Color temperature measures the relative reddishness and bluishness of white light. | 9 ○ 114 | ○ 115 |
| **10.** | In most cases, a reflector can substitute for a fill light. | 10 ○ 116 | ○ 117 |
| **11.** | Plugging portable lights into different wall outlets means that they are automatically on different power circuits. | 11 ○ 118 | ○ 119 |
| **12.** | Cast shadows can suggest a specific locale. | 12 ○ 120 | ○ 121 |

SECTION
TOTAL ☐

<br>

## PROBLEM-SOLVING APPLICATIONS

1. You are asked to do the lighting for a shampoo commercial. The director wants you to make the model's blond hair look especially brilliant and glamorous. Which of the three instruments of the lighting triangle needs special attention to achieve the desired result?

2. The show is a brief address by the CEO. Prepare a light plot for the floor plan shown below. Sketch the type and locations of the instruments used, as well as the general direction of the light beams.

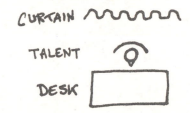

CURTAIN

TALENT

DESK

3. You (the camera operator) and a field reporter are sent by the assignment editor to the Plaza Hotel to interview a famous soprano in her room. The field reporter will remain off-camera during the interview. The lighting in the hotel room is inadequate, so you need additional lighting. Besides the camera light, you have only one Omni light at your disposal. Where would you place the Omni light? Why?

4. You are the LD for an indoor springtime fashion show. The studio audience is seated along both sides of the runway. The novice director suggests low-key lighting to give the show some extra sparkle. Do you agree with the director's suggestion? If so, why? If not, why not? What are your recommendations?

5. You are the LD for a dance number. The dancers wear off-white leotards. The choreographer wants them to appear first in cameo, then as illuminated figures against a dark blue background, and then, in one continuous take, as black silhouettes moving against a bright red background. Can you fulfill the choreographer's request? If so, how? If not, why not?

6. You will be shooting an interview with the CEO of a large software company. Her office has a large window without any curtains. How would you light this interview while taking advantage of the daylight coming through the window? List specific lights, their locations, and all necessary support equipment.

7. You are covering a dedication of a new library. It is a cloudless, sunny day with the sun reflecting off the brilliantly white building. The dedication is planned to happen right in front of the building. What are your concerns regarding lighting? What would you suggest to minimize some of the problems?

8. You are to light a two-anchor news set in which the two co-anchors (a dark-haired man and a blond woman) sit side-by-side. The man is worried about his wrinkles, especially because his co-anchor has perfectly smooth skin. What lighting would you suggest? Draw a rough light plot that indicates the type and approximate locations of the instruments used.

# 9 Audio: Sound Pickup

## REVIEW OF KEY TERMS

*Match each term with its appropriate definition by filling in the corresponding bubble.*

1. cardioid
2. flat response
3. ribbon microphone
4. polar pattern
5. pickup pattern
6. condenser microphone
7. dynamic microphone
8. unidirectional
9. omnidirectional
10. impedance
11. frequency response

**A.** A microphone whose sound pickup device consists of a thin band that vibrates with the sound pressures within a magnetic field.

A
1 2 3 4
5 6 7 8
9 10 11

**B.** A microphone whose diaphragm consists of a plate that vibrates with the sound pressure against another fixed plate (the backplate).

B
1 2 3 4
5 6 7 8
9 10 11

**C.** A type of pickup pattern in which the microphone can pick up sounds better from one direction—the front—than from the sides or back.

C
1 2 3 4
5 6 7 8
9 10 11

PAGE TOTAL

© 2006 Thomson Wadsworth

| 1. cardioid | 5. pickup pattern | 9. omnidirectional |
| 2. flat response | 6. condenser microphone | 10. impedance |
| 3. ribbon microphone | 7. dynamic microphone | 11. frequency response |
| 4. polar pattern | 8. unidirectional | |

**D.** A type of pickup pattern in which the microphone can pick up sounds equally well from all directions.

D  ◯ ◯ ◯ ◯
   1  2  3  4
  ◯ ◯ ◯ ◯
   5  6  7  8
  ◯ ◯ ◯
   9  10  11

**E.** A microphone whose sound pickup device consists of a diaphragm that is attached to a movable coil.

E  ◯ ◯ ◯ ◯
   1  2  3  4
  ◯ ◯ ◯ ◯
   5  6  7  8
  ◯ ◯ ◯
   9  10  11

**F.** The range of frequencies a microphone can hear and reproduce.

F  ◯ ◯ ◯ ◯
   1  2  3  4
  ◯ ◯ ◯ ◯
   5  6  7  8
  ◯ ◯ ◯
   9  10  11

**G.** The territory around the microphone within which the microphone can "hear" well, or has optimal sound pickup.

G  ◯ ◯ ◯ ◯
   1  2  3  4
  ◯ ◯ ◯ ◯
   5  6  7  8
  ◯ ◯ ◯
   9  10  11

**H.** A specific pickup pattern of unidirectional microphones.

H  ◯ ◯ ◯ ◯
   1  2  3  4
  ◯ ◯ ◯ ◯
   5  6  7  8
  ◯ ◯ ◯
   9  10  11

PAGE TOTAL _____

*Chapter 9 — Audio: Sound Pickup*

| | | |
|---|---|---|
| 1. cardioid | 5. pickup pattern | 9. omnidirectional |
| 2. flat response | 6. condenser microphone | 10. impedance |
| 3. ribbon microphone | 7. dynamic microphone | 11. frequency response |
| 4. polar pattern | 8. unidirectional | |

**I.** The measure of a microphone's ability to hear equally well over its entire frequency range.

**I**  ○ ○ ○ ○
   1  2  3  4
   ○ ○ ○ ○
   5  6  7  8
   ○ ○ ○
   9 10 11

**J.** A type of resistance to a signal flow: high-Z or low-Z.

**J**  ○ ○ ○ ○
   1  2  3  4
   ○ ○ ○ ○
   5  6  7  8
   ○ ○ ○
   9 10 11

**K.** The two-dimensional representation of a microphone pickup pattern.

**K**  ○ ○ ○ ○
   1  2  3  4
   ○ ○ ○ ○
   5  6  7  8
   ○ ○ ○
   9 10 11

PAGE TOTAL ☐

SECTION TOTAL ☐

## REVIEW OF ELECTRONIC CHARACTERISTICS OF MICROPHONES

1. Fill in the bubbles whose numbers correspond with the polar patterns in the figure below.

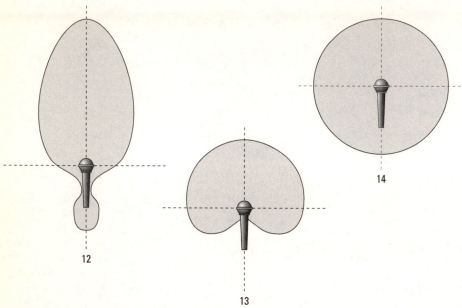

12

13

14

**a.** omnidirectional

**b.** cardioid

**c.** hypercardioid

*Select the correct answers and fill in the bubbles with the corresponding numbers.*

2. Select the three types of microphones as classified by their generating element: (15) *dynamic* (16) *unidirectional* (17) *cardioid* (18) *ribbon* (19) *hypercardioid* (20) *condenser.* **(Fill in three bubbles.)**

3. To eliminate sudden breath pops when speaking close to the microphone, we use a (21) *pop filter* (22) *windscreen* (23) *frequency filter.*

4. In general, dynamic microphones are (24) *more rugged than* (25) *less rugged than* (26) *equally sensitive as* ribbon microphones.

5. Normally, shotgun microphones have (27) *an omnidirectional* (28) *an extremely directional* (29) *a nondirectional* pickup pattern.

| 1a | ○ 12 | ○ 13 | ○ 14 |
| 1b | ○ 12 | ○ 13 | ○ 14 |
| 1c | ○ 12 | ○ 13 | ○ 14 |
| 2 | ○ 15 | ○ 16 | ○ 17 |
|   | ○ 18 | ○ 19 | ○ 20 |
| 3 | ○ 21 | ○ 22 | ○ 23 |
| 4 | ○ 24 | ○ 25 | ○ 26 |
| 5 | ○ 27 | ○ 28 | ○ 29 |

SECTION TOTAL

Course No. _____  Date _____  Name _____

## REVIEW OF OPERATIONAL CHARACTERISTICS OF MICROPHONES

*Select the correct answers and fill in the bubbles with the corresponding numbers.*

1. A shotgun microphone attached to a fishpole or perambulator has (30) *an omnidirectional* (31) *a cardioid* (32) *a hyper- or supercardioid* pickup pattern.

2. Two high-quality hand microphones that are normally used for music pickup in the studio are (33) *dynamic* (34) *ribbon* (35) *condenser.* **(Fill in two bubbles.)**

3. The hand microphones used in ENG normally have (36) *an omnidirectional* (37) *a cardioid* (38) *a hyper- or supercardioid* pickup pattern.

4. The most rugged ENG hand mics have a (39) *dynamic* (40) *ribbon* (41) *condenser* sound-generating element.

5. The microphones that are most appropriate for voice pickup of a four-member news team (two anchors, a weathercaster, and a sportscaster) are (42) *boom mics* (43) *desk mics* (44) *lavalieres.*

6. You are to set up microphones for a six-member panel discussion. All participants sit in a row at a table. Normally, you would use (45) *boom mics* (46) *hand mics* (47) *desk mics* for this production.

7. When setting up the microphones for a panel show, the audio engineer advises you to place the mics in such a way that they will not cause "multiple-microphone interference." This means that the mics must be placed so that they will not (48) *block the faces of the panel members* (49) *cancel some of one another's frequencies* (50) *multiply the ambient noise.*

8. To achieve a good and efficient voice pickup during the videotaping of four people sitting around a table in a rather small office, talking about effective sound handling in ENG/EFP, you should use (51) *a large shotgun mic* (52) *a boundary mic* (53) *a parabolic reflector mic.*

9. A microphone that hears equally well over the entire frequency range has a (54) *flat response* (55) *balanced signal* (56) *low impedance.*

10. Parabolic microphones are especially effective for picking up (57) *extremely close sounds* (58) *especially soft sounds* (59) *faraway sounds.*

11. When doing a live report from an accident scene, the most practical mic is a (60) *lavaliere mic* (61) *hand mic* (62) *boom mic.*

Answer bubbles:
1. ○30 ○31 ○32
2. ○33 ○34 ○35
3. ○36 ○37 ○38
4. ○39 ○40 ○41
5. ○42 ○43 ○44
6. ○45 ○46 ○47
7. ○48 ○49 ○50
8. ○51 ○52 ○53
9. ○54 ○55 ○56
10. ○57 ○58 ○59
11. ○60 ○61 ○62

SECTION TOTAL [   ]

© 2006 Thomson Wadsworth

## REVIEW QUIZ

*Mark the following statements as true or false by filling in the bubbles in the* **T** *(for true) or* **F** *(for false) column.*

|  |  | T | F |
|---|---|---|---|
| **1.** | A windsock fulfills the identical function as a pop filter. | **1** ○ 63 | ○ 64 |
| **2.** | A balanced mic cable is less susceptible to electronic interference than an unbalanced one. | **2** ○ 65 | ○ 66 |
| **3.** | All professional microphones use three-pronged XLR connectors. | **3** ○ 67 | ○ 68 |
| **4.** | Dynamic mics are generally less sensitive to shock and temperature extremes than ribbon mics. | **4** ○ 69 | ○ 70 |
| **5.** | Because the boundary, or pressure zone, microphone needs a sound-reflecting surface, it cannot be used as a hanging mic. | **5** ○ 71 | ○ 72 |
| **6.** | Because wireless microphones operate on their own frequency, they are totally immune to interference from other radio frequencies. | **6** ○ 73 | ○ 74 |
| **7.** | The parabolic reflector microphone is especially appropriate for intimate, high-quality sound pickup with a high degree of sound presence. | **7** ○ 75 | ○ 76 |
| **8.** | Blowing into a microphone is a good way to test whether it is turned on. | **8** ○ 77 | ○ 78 |
| **9.** | Dual redundancy allows a backup microphone in case a microphone fails. | **9** ○ 79 | ○ 80 |
| **10.** | Using an impedance transformer (direct box) allows you to play an electric guitar into a mixer. | **10** ○ 81 | ○ 82 |
| **11.** | Because lavaliere microphones are highly sensitive, they work best when hidden under a shirt or blouse. | **11** ○ 83 | ○ 84 |
| **12.** | A hand mic clipped to a desk stand can serve as a desk mic. | **12** ○ 85 | ○ 86 |
| **13.** | Ribbon mics are especially good for the pickup of a bass drum. | **13** ○ 87 | ○ 88 |

SECTION TOTAL

## PROBLEM-SOLVING APPLICATIONS

1. You are to provide optimal sound pickup for a preschool children's live-on-tape show. The show consists of a host who moves among five to seven children seated on little chairs. The chairs are grouped around a small rug on which the children also play or dance from time to time. The dance music and other recorded audio portions are piped into the studio through the S.A. system. What microphone setup would you suggest for the host and the children? What problems might the S.A. system cause, if any?

2. You are in charge of audio for a show that consists of several intimate numbers by a singer and a small band. After the rehearsal, an observer in the control room tells you that the singer holds the mic much too close to her mouth and that she should hold the mic lower and sing *across* rather than *into* it. What is your reaction? Why?

3. You are responsible for audio pickup for the live remote coverage at the airport during the Thanksgiving rush. Basically, you will have a host walking among the people waiting at the ticket counters, briefly interviewing some of the travelers. What type of mic would you use? Why?

4. An official at your former high school asks you to help with the audio for the championship basketball game. Somehow, so the official claims, the visiting spectators seem much louder on television than the home audience, although the latter is actually much larger and noisier than the guests. What can you do to accurately reflect the supportive cheering of the two sides? What specific microphone setups would you use?

5. You are doing a documentary on police patrols in your city. You first want to hear the conversation and the police radio inside the patrol car and then capture the sounds of conversations, yelling, or any other audio when the officers leave the patrol car to confront a suspect. What microphones would you need for optimal sound pickup in these situations?

6. You are to conduct an interview with the university president in her office. What microphones would you use? Why?

# 10 Audio: Sound Control

## ■ REVIEW OF KEY TERMS

*Match each term with its appropriate definition by filling in the corresponding bubble.*

1. AGC
2. mix-minus
3. ADR
4. digital cart system
5. VU meter
6. equalization
7. sweetening
8. MIDI
9. figure/ground
10. calibration

**A.** Controlling the audio signal by emphasizing certain frequencies and eliminating others.

A  ○ ○ ○ ○ ○
   1  2  3  4  5
   ○ ○ ○ ○ ○
   6  7  8  9  10

**B.** Regulates the audio or video levels automatically, without using pots.

B  ○ ○ ○ ○ ○
   1  2  3  4  5
   ○ ○ ○ ○ ○
   6  7  8  9  10

**C.** A variety of quality adjustments of recorded sound in postproduction.

C  ○ ○ ○ ○ ○
   1  2  3  4  5
   ○ ○ ○ ○ ○
   6  7  8  9  10

**D.** Emphasizing the most important sound source over other sounds.

D  ○ ○ ○ ○ ○
   1  2  3  4  5
   ○ ○ ○ ○ ○
   6  7  8  9  10

**E.** Audio feed missing the part that is being recorded.

E  ○ ○ ○ ○ ○
   1  2  3  4  5
   ○ ○ ○ ○ ○
   6  7  8  9  10

PAGE TOTAL [      ]

1. AGC
2. mix-minus
3. ADR
4. digital cart system

5. VU meter
6. equalization
7. sweetening

8. MIDI
9. figure/ground
10. calibration

**F.** Making all VU meters respond in the same way to a specific audio signal.

F
○ ○ ○ ○ ○
1 2 3 4 5
○ ○ ○ ○ ○
6 7 8 9 10

**G.** A standardization device (cable) that allows the interfacing of various digital audio equipment.

G
○ ○ ○ ○ ○
1 2 3 4 5
○ ○ ○ ○ ○
6 7 8 9 10

**H.** The postproduction synchronization of speech with the lip movement of the speaker.

H
○ ○ ○ ○ ○
1 2 3 4 5
○ ○ ○ ○ ○
6 7 8 9 10

**I.** Normally used for the playback of brief announcements and music bridges.

I
○ ○ ○ ○ ○
1 2 3 4 5
○ ○ ○ ○ ○
6 7 8 9 10

**J.** Measures volume units, the relative loudness of sound.

J
○ ○ ○ ○ ○
1 2 3 4 5
○ ○ ○ ○ ○
6 7 8 9 10

PAGE
TOTAL

SECTION
TOTAL

## REVIEW OF AUDIO EQUIPMENT AND FUNCTIONS

*Select the correct answers and fill in the bubbles with the corresponding numbers.*

**1.** In a patch panel, the jacks that carry the signal from mics, CDs, and ATRs are called (11) *outputs* (12) *inputs* (13) *the mix bus.*

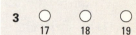

**2.** The CD-RW (14) *records and plays analog audio signals* (15) *can be used for repeated recording and playback of digital audio signals* (16) *only plays digital audio signals.*

**3.** Indicate the most common place to cut the digital audio track shown below:

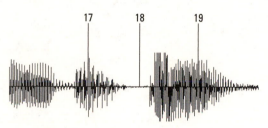

**4.** A television audio console will allow you to (20) *synchronize audio and video tracks in postproduction* (21) *punch up the video source with the corresponding audio* (22) *adjust the volume of the incoming audio signals.*

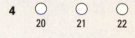

**5.** The appropriate place that marks the beginning of the "overload zone" is (23) *–5 VU* (24) *–2 VU* (25) *0 VU.*

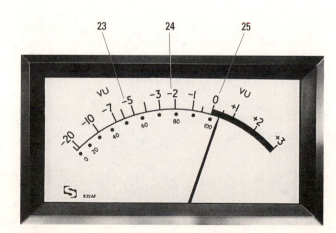

| | | |
|---|---|---|
| **1** ○ 11 | ○ 12 | ○ 13 |
| **2** ○ 14 | ○ 15 | ○ 16 |
| **3** ○ 17 | ○ 18 | ○ 19 |
| **4** ○ 20 | ○ 21 | ○ 22 |
| **5** ○ 23 | ○ 24 | ○ 25 |

PAGE TOTAL [ ]

**6.** Fill in the bubble whose number identifies the type of head in the following head assembly:

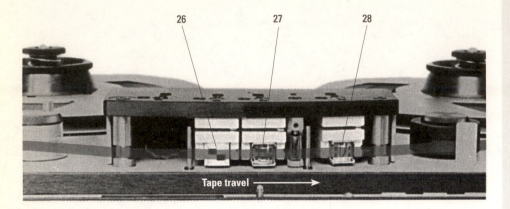

26    27    28

Tape travel ⟶

**a.** playback head

**b.** record head

**c.** erase head

**7.** When using a CD player as an audio source, the mic/line input on the mixer must be switched to (29) *mic* (30) *line* (31) *neither.*

**8.** Most software programs for digital audio/video synchronization let you (32) *only see the audio track* (33) *only hear the audio track* (34) *see and hear the audio track.*

**9.** A 16 × 2 audio console has (35) *sixteen inputs and two outputs* (36) *sixteen slide faders and two monitor systems* (37) *sixteen VU meters and two mix buses.*

**10.** Phantom power means that the power is (38) *virtual but not real* (39) *not necessary* (40) *not supplied by battery but by some other source.*

| | | | |
|---|---|---|---|
| **6a** | ○ 26 | ○ 27 | ○ 28 |
| **6b** | ○ 26 | ○ 27 | ○ 28 |
| **6c** | ○ 26 | ○ 27 | ○ 28 |
| **7** | ○ 29 | ○ 30 | ○ 31 |
| **8** | ○ 32 | ○ 33 | ○ 34 |
| **9** | ○ 35 | ○ 36 | ○ 37 |
| **10** | ○ 38 | ○ 39 | ○ 40 |

PAGE TOTAL

SECTION TOTAL

Course No. _____  Date _____  Name _____

## REVIEW OF AUDIO OPERATION AND AESTHETICS

*Select the correct answers and fill in the bubbles with the corresponding numbers.*

**1.** The correct patches as shown in the figure are:
(41) (42) (43) (44) (45) (46). *(Multiple answers are possible.)*

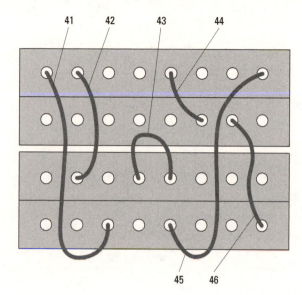

**1**  ○ 41  ○ 42  ○ 43
      ○ 44  ○ 45  ○ 46

**2.** The audio control tone, which gives a reference level of the recorded material, should be set at (47) *0 VU* (48) *+3 VU* (49) *–3 VU.*

**2**  ○ 47  ○ 48  ○ 49

**3.** Sound perspective means (50) *the directionality between the left and right channels in stereo audio* (51) *close-ups go with close sound, long shots with faraway sounds* (52) *the sound presence does not change regardless of the field of view.*

**3**  ○ 50  ○ 51  ○ 52

**4.** When recording sound during an outdoor EFP, you should (53) *avoid all ambient sounds* (54) *record ambient sounds on a separate track* (55) *re-create all sounds in postproduction.*

**4**  ○ 53  ○ 54  ○ 55

**5.** The AGC (56) *discriminates automatically between figure and ground* (57) *works especially well in noisy surroundings* (58) *automatically boosts audio levels if they fall below preset levels.*

**5**  ○ 56  ○ 57  ○ 58

**6.** Audio-system calibration normally refers to (59) *adjusting the audio input VU meter of the VTR to the VU meter of the console output* (60) *adjusting the zoom lens so that it stays in focus* (61) *having the VU meter of the VTR peak at a much higher level than the VU meter of the console output.*

**6**  ○ 59  ○ 60  ○ 61

PAGE TOTAL [ ]

© 2006 Thomson Wadsworth

**7.** Recording environmental sounds is especially important during  (62) *ENG*
(63) *studio drama*  (64) *studio taping of a string quartet.*

**8.** The flash memory device (flash drive) can store  (65) *analog*  (66) *digital*
(67) *both types of* audio signals.

**9.** The proper steps for audio system calibration are:

    (68) *1. Activate the control tone on the console or mixer.*
       *2. Turn up the volume control for the incoming sound on the VTR to 0 VU.*
       *3. Bring up the control tone fader on the console (mixer) to 0 VU.*
       *4. Bring up the master fader on the console or mixer to 0 VU.*

    (69) *1. Turn up the volume control for the incoming sound on the VTR to 0 VU.*
       *2. Bring up the control tone fader on the console (mixer) to 0 VU.*
       *3. Bring up the master fader on the console or mixer to 0 VU.*
       *4. Activate the control tone on the console or mixer.*

    (70) *1. Activate the control tone on the console or mixer.*
       *2. Bring up the master fader on the console or mixer to 0 VU.*
       *3. Bring up the control tone fader on the console (mixer) to 0 VU.*
       *4. Turn up the volume control for the incoming sound on the VTR to 0 VU.*

**10.** Taking a level is  (71) *not necessary when the AGC is engaged*  (72) *not
necessary when recording digital sound*  (73) *always necessary.*

## REVIEW QUIZ

*Mark the following statements as true or false by filling in the bubbles in the* **T** *(for true) or* **F** *(for false) column.*

|  |  | T | F |
|---|---|---|---|
| 1. | The VU meter or the PPM will give an accurate reading of sound perspective. | 1 ○ 74 | ○ 75 |
| 2. | Mix-minus and foldback are identical audio production techniques. | 2 ○ 76 | ○ 77 |
| 3. | Environmental sounds are always interfering in EFP. | 3 ○ 78 | ○ 79 |
| 4. | MIDI is a computer that translates analog audio signals into digital form. | 4 ○ 80 | ○ 81 |
| 5. | Some digital audiotape recorders use videotape mechanisms to record multitrack audio signals. | 5 ○ 82 | ○ 83 |
| 6. | On multitrack ATRs each track has its own VU meter. | 6 ○ 84 | ○ 85 |
| 7. | In EFP we should try to mix all sound inputs as much as possible to minimize the need for postproduction mixing. | 7 ○ 86 | ○ 87 |
| 8. | I/O consoles have the same number of outputs as inputs. | 8 ○ 88 | ○ 89 |
| 9. | On large multichannel consoles, each input channel has its own quality controls. | 9 ○ 90 | ○ 91 |
| 10. | In contrast to large audio consoles, audio mixers have only one input but several outputs. | 10 ○ 92 | ○ 93 |
| 11. | All analog recording systems are tape-based. | 11 ○ 94 | ○ 95 |
| 12. | Digital audio signals can be recorded on tape or various computer disks. | 12 ○ 96 | ○ 97 |

SECTION TOTAL [ ]

## PROBLEM-SOLVING APPLICATIONS

1. When setting up for videotaping a small rock group, you notice that the microphones and other audio sources exceed the number of inputs on the audio console. What can you do?

2. During rehearsal of the same production, you discover that the audio inputs that need the most attention are widely spread apart on the board. How can you get them closer together on the console so that their respective volume controls are adjacent to one another?

3. During the digital recording of a concert, the VU meters occasionally peak into the +2 red zone. The director is very concerned about overmodulation. What is your response?

4. During a small segment of an EFP in an auto assembly plant, the novice director tells you to be especially careful to mix the ambient sounds and the voices of the reporter and the plant supervisor with the portable mixer so as to facilitate postproduction editing. What is your response?

5. You, the audio technician, overhear the floor manager telling the anchorpersons that they do not need to be on the I.F.B. system because it is, after all, his job to relay messages to the talent. What is your response?

6. You have been asked to calibrate the audio system in your studio. Briefly describe the process step-by-step.

# 11 Switching, or Instantaneous Editing

---

## REVIEW OF KEY TERMS

*Match each term with its appropriate definition by filling in the corresponding bubble.*

1. preview/
   preset bus
2. program bus
3. M/E bus
4. wipe patterns

5. fader bar
6. delegation controls
7. downstream keyer (DSK)
8. take, or cut, button

9. key-level control, or clipper
10. key bus
11. auto transition

**A.** Control that allows a title to be keyed over the line-out image as it leaves the switcher.

A  ○ ○ ○ ○
   1 2 3 4
   ○ ○ ○ ○
   5 6 7 8
   ○ ○ ○
   9 10 11

**B.** A row of buttons that show different geometric transition shapes.

B  ○ ○ ○ ○
   1 2 3 4
   ○ ○ ○ ○
   5 6 7 8
   ○ ○ ○
   9 10 11

**C.** Rows of buttons used to select the upcoming video and route it to the preview monitor.

C  ○ ○ ○ ○
   1 2 3 4
   ○ ○ ○ ○
   5 6 7 8
   ○ ○ ○
   9 10 11

PAGE
TOTAL [   ]

| | | |
|---|---|---|
| 1. preview/<br>preset bus | 5. fader bar | 9. key-level control,<br>or clipper |
| 2. program bus | 6. delegation controls | 10. key bus |
| 3. M/E bus | 7. downstream keyer<br>(DSK) | 11. auto transition |
| 4. wipe patterns | 8. take, or cut, button | |

**D.** When activated, will switch instantly from the on-line picture to the preset one.

D
○ ○ ○ ○
1 2 3 4
○ ○ ○ ○
5 6 7 8
○ ○ ○
9 10 11

**E.** A row of buttons that can serve a mix or an effects function.

E
○ ○ ○ ○
1 2 3 4
○ ○ ○ ○
5 6 7 8
○ ○ ○
9 10 11

**F.** A button that triggers the functions of a fader bar.

F
○ ○ ○ ○
1 2 3 4
○ ○ ○ ○
5 6 7 8
○ ○ ○
9 10 11

**G.** Adjusts the signal doing the cutting so that the title to be inserted appears sharp and clear.

G
○ ○ ○ ○
1 2 3 4
○ ○ ○ ○
5 6 7 8
○ ○ ○
9 10 11

**H.** The bus on a switcher whose inputs are directly switched to the line-out.

H
○ ○ ○ ○
1 2 3 4
○ ○ ○ ○
5 6 7 8
○ ○ ○
9 10 11

PAGE
TOTAL

---

| | | |
|---|---|---|
| 1. preview/ preset bus | 5. fader bar | 9. key-level control, or clipper |
| 2. program bus | 6. delegation controls | 10. key bus |
| 3. M/E bus | 7. downstream keyer (DSK) | 11. auto transition |
| 4. wipe patterns | 8. take, or cut, button | |

---

**I.**   A lever on the switcher that activates preset functions such as dissolves, fades, and wipes of varying speeds.

I
○ ○ ○ ○
1  2  3  4
○ ○ ○ ○
5  6  7  8
○ ○ ○
9 10 11

**J.**   Controls on a switcher that assign specific functions to a bus.

J
○ ○ ○ ○
1  2  3  4
○ ○ ○ ○
5  6  7  8
○ ○ ○
9 10 11

**K.**   A bus used to select the video source to be inserted into a background image.

K
○ ○ ○ ○
1  2  3  4
○ ○ ○ ○
5  6  7  8
○ ○ ○
9 10 11

PAGE TOTAL [        ]

SECTION TOTAL [        ]

# REVIEW OF BASIC SWITCHER LAYOUT AND OPERATION

1. Fill in the bubbles whose numbers correspond with the appropriate parts of the switcher shown in the following figure.

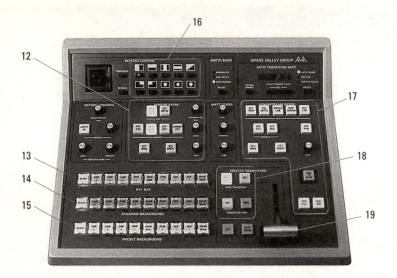

**a.** program bus

**b.** preview/preset bus

**c.** fader bar

**d.** key bus

**e.** delegation controls (mix/effects transition)

**f.** wipe pattern selector

**g.** downstream keyer controls

**h.** key/matte controls

**1a** ◯ ◯ ◯ ◯
   12  13  14  15
   ◯ ◯ ◯ ◯
   16  17  18  19

**1b** ◯ ◯ ◯ ◯
   12  13  14  15
   ◯ ◯ ◯ ◯
   16  17  18  19

**1c** ◯ ◯ ◯ ◯
   12  13  14  15
   ◯ ◯ ◯ ◯
   16  17  18  19

**1d** ◯ ◯ ◯ ◯
   12  13  14  15
   ◯ ◯ ◯ ◯
   16  17  18  19

**1e** ◯ ◯ ◯ ◯
   12  13  14  15
   ◯ ◯ ◯ ◯
   16  17  18  19

**1f** ◯ ◯ ◯ ◯
   12  13  14  15
   ◯ ◯ ◯ ◯
   16  17  18  19

**1g** ◯ ◯ ◯ ◯
   12  13  14  15
   ◯ ◯ ◯ ◯
   16  17  18  19

**1h** ◯ ◯ ◯ ◯
   12  13  14  15
   ◯ ◯ ◯ ◯
   16  17  18  19

PAGE
TOTAL

*Select the correct answers and fill in the bubbles with the corresponding numbers.*

2. To switch from C1 (camera 1) to C3 by pressing only one button, you need to press the (20) *C3 button on the preset bus* (21) *C3 button on the key bus* (22) *C3 button on the program bus.* **(This assumes that the appropriate buses have already been delegated a mix/effects function.)**

2   ○ 20   ○ 21   ○ 22

3. To dissolve from C3 to VTR (with the auto transition in the *off* position), you (23) *press the VTR button on the preset bus, then press the cut button* (24) *press the VTR button on the preset bus, then move the fader bar to the opposite position* (25) *press the VTR button on the key bus, then move the fader bar to the opposite position.*

3   ○ 23   ○ 24   ○ 25

4. The program bus will direct the selected video source to the (26) *preview monitor* (27) *mix bus* (28) *line-out.*

4   ○ 26   ○ 27   ○ 28

5. To have C3 appear on the preview monitor before switching to it from C1, you need to (29) *press C3 on the preset bus* (30) *press C3 on the preset bus, then press the key button* (31) *press C3 on the program bus, then move the fader bar to the opposite position.*

5   ○ 29   ○ 30   ○ 31

6. To select the functions of a specific bus or buses, you need to activate the (32) *joystick* (33) *wipe mode selectors* (34) *delegation controls.*

6   ○ 32   ○ 33   ○ 34

7. Assuming that the final C.G. credits are keyed with the DSK, you can go to black by (35) *pressing the black button on the program bus* (36) *pressing the black button on the key bus* (37) *pressing the black button in the downstream keyer section.*

7   ○ 35   ○ 36   ○ 37

P A G E
T O T A L [ ]

© 2006 Thomson Wadsworth

**8.** Identify the proper preview and line monitor images you would expect to see from the switcher output by filling in the corresponding bubble. The highlighted buttons on the following switcher have already been pressed. C1 is focused on the host, C2 on the dancers (see the monitor images below).

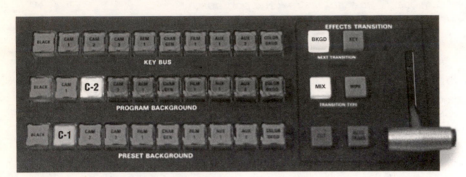

38

Preview

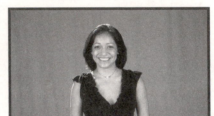

Line

39

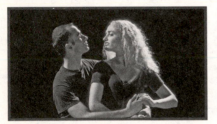

Preview

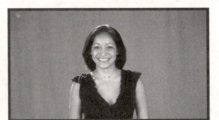

Line

40

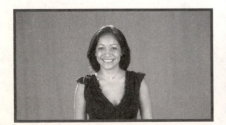

Preview

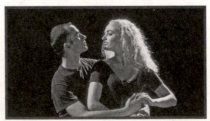

Line

PAGE TOTAL

*Chapter 11* — *Switching, or Instantaneous Editing*

**9.** Identify the proper preview and line monitor images you would expect to see from the switcher output and fill in the corresponding bubble.

**9** ◯ ◯ ◯
   41 42 43

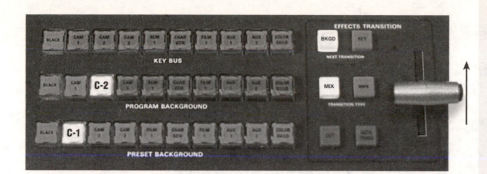

41
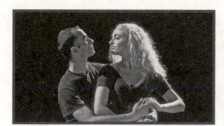
Preview
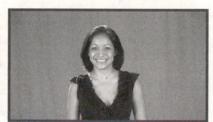
Line

42
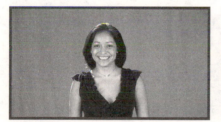
Preview
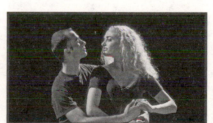
Line

43
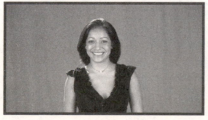
Preview
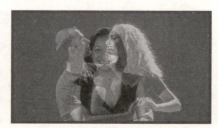
Line

PAGE TOTAL

*Chapter 11* — *Switching, or Instantaneous Editing*

**10.** Identify the proper preview and line monitor images you would expect to see from the switcher output at the end of the previous dissolve and fill in the corresponding bubble.

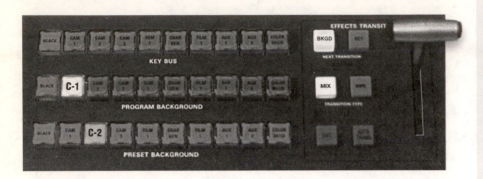

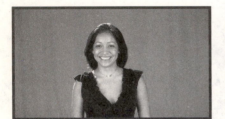

44

Preview

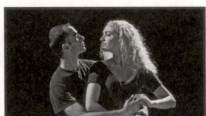

Line

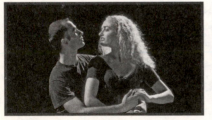

45

Preview

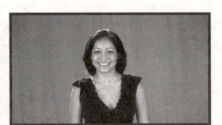

Line

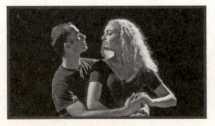

46

Preview

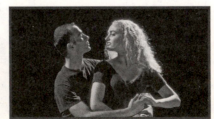

Line

## REVIEW QUIZ

*Mark the following statements as true or false by filling in the bubbles in the*
*T (for true) or F (for false) column.*

|   |   | T | F |
|---|---|---|---|

1. The clip control allows you to adjust the hue and the saturation on the image selected on the program bus.

     **1** ◯ 47   ◯ 48

2. Through delegation controls, you can assign a preview function to the program bus.

     **2** ◯ 49   ◯ 50

3. It is impossible to have both preset and program buses activated at the same time.

     **3** ◯ 51   ◯ 52

4. The downstream keyer can add a title key only if there are no other keys present in the line-out picture.

     **4** ◯ 53   ◯ 54

5. The auto transition fulfills the same function as the fader bar.

     **5** ◯ 55   ◯ 56

6. The switcher has a separate button for each video input.

     **6** ◯ 57   ◯ 58

7. The preview bus can also be used as a mix bus, if so delegated.

     **7** ◯ 59   ◯ 60

8. Everything that is punched up on the program bus will go directly to the line-out.

     **8** ◯ 61   ◯ 62

9. Assuming that you are not using auto transition, the speed of a dissolve depends on how fast the fader bar is moved up or down.

     **9** ◯ 63   ◯ 64

10. The DSK black button will put the switcher output to black regardless of what source feeds the line-out.

     **10** ◯ 65   ◯ 66

**SECTION TOTAL** [　　　]

*Chapter 11 — Switching, or Instantaneous Editing*

1. Assuming that you operate the Grass Valley 100 switcher shown below (or a switcher with a similar architecture), can you add a second title key even though the regular key bus is already in use with a key? If so, how? If not, why not?

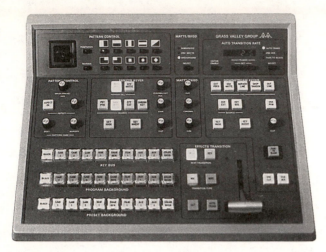

2. The director asks you, the TD, to superimpose a long shot of a dancer over a close-up of her face. The director wants to first have the long shot be the more prominent image and then slowly shift the emphasis to the close-up. How, if at all, can you accomplish such an effect?

3. The director wants you to perform four dissolves that are identical in speed from one dancer to the next. Are such identical dissolves possible? If so, how can they be accomplished? If not, why not?

4. You have keyed the credits over the base picture with the downstream keyer. When the director calls for a fade to black, you press the black button on the program bus. What will you see on the line monitor? Why?

5. The director wants you to cut between the CUs of the interviewer and the guest during a lively discussion. How can you best accomplish such fast cuts to the person who is doing the talking?

# 12 Video-recording and Storage Systems

## REVIEW OF KEY TERMS

*Match each term with its appropriate definition by filling in the corresponding bubble.*

1. **TBC**
2. **composite, or NTSC, system**
3. **Y/C component system**
4. **control track**
5. **Y/color difference component system**
6. **compression**
7. **disk-based VR**
8. **FireWire or i-link**
9. **framestore synchronizer**
10. **MPEG-2**
11. **flash memory device**

**A.** A small read/write solid-state digital storage medium that uses no disk.

A    ① ② ③ ④    1 2 3 4
     ⑤ ⑥ ⑦ ⑧    5 6 7 8
     ⑨ ⑩ ⑪    9 10 11

**B.** A cable that can transfer digital signals from a camcorder to a computer hard disk.

B    ① ② ③ ④    1 2 3 4
     ⑤ ⑥ ⑦ ⑧    5 6 7 8
     ⑨ ⑩ ⑪    9 10 11

**C.** All digital VRs that record or store information on a hard drive or read/write optical disc.

C    ① ② ③ ④    1 2 3 4
     ⑤ ⑥ ⑦ ⑧    5 6 7 8
     ⑨ ⑩ ⑪    9 10 11

PAGE TOTAL [    ]

| 1. TBC | 5. Y/color difference component system | 9. framestore synchronizer |
| 2. composite, or NTSC, system | 6. compression | 10. MPEG-2 |
| 3. Y/C component system | 7. disk-based VR | 11. flash memory device |
| 4. control track | 8. FireWire or i-link | |

**D.** A system in which the luminance (Y), and the R–Y and B–Y signals are kept separate throughout the video-recording process.

D ○ ○ ○ ○
  1 2 3 4
  ○ ○ ○ ○
  5 6 7 8
  ○ ○ ○
  9 10 11

**E.** A compression system generally used for digital television.

E ○ ○ ○ ○
  1 2 3 4
  ○ ○ ○ ○
  5 6 7 8
  ○ ○ ○
  9 10 11

**F.** Electronic accessory to a VTR that makes playbacks or transfers stable.

F ○ ○ ○ ○
  1 2 3 4
  ○ ○ ○ ○
  5 6 7 8
  ○ ○ ○
  9 10 11

**G.** A video signal in which luminance (Y), chrominance (C), and sync information are encoded into a single signal.

G ○ ○ ○ ○
  1 2 3 4
  ○ ○ ○ ○
  5 6 7 8
  ○ ○ ○
  9 10 11

**H.** Image stabilization and synchronization system that stores and reads out one complete video frame.

H ○ ○ ○ ○
  1 2 3 4
  ○ ○ ○ ○
  5 6 7 8
  ○ ○ ○
  9 10 11

PAGE TOTAL [ ]

| | | |
|---|---|---|
| 1. **TBC** | 5. **Y/color difference component system** | 9. **framestore synchronizer** |
| 2. **composite, or NTSC, system** | 6. **compression** | 10. **MPEG-2** |
| 3. **Y/C component system** | 7. **disk-based VR** | 11. **flash memory device** |
| 4. **control track** | 8. **FireWire or i-link** | |

**I.** The track on a videotape that contains synchronization information.

I ○ ○ ○ ○  1 2 3 4  ○ ○ ○ ○  5 6 7 8  ○ ○ ○  9 10 11

**J.** Reducing the amount of digital data for recording or transmission.

J ○ ○ ○ ○  1 2 3 4  ○ ○ ○ ○  5 6 7 8  ○ ○ ○  9 10 11

**K.** A system in which the luminance (Y) and chrominance (C) signals are kept separate during the encoding and decoding processes but are recorded together.

K ○ ○ ○ ○  1 2 3 4  ○ ○ ○ ○  5 6 7 8  ○ ○ ○  9 10 11

PAGE TOTAL

SECTION TOTAL

© 2006 Thomson Wadsworth

*Chapter 12* — *Video-recording and Storage Systems*

## REVIEW OF TAPE- AND DISK-BASED RECORDING SYSTEMS

*Select the correct answers and fill in the bubbles with the corresponding numbers.*

**1.** Digital recording systems can be (12) *linear* (13) *nonlinear* (14) *linear or nonlinear, depending on the recording system.*

**1** ◯ 12 ◯ 13 ◯ 14

**2.** Disk-based recording systems are always (15) *linear* (16) *nonlinear* (17) *linear and nonlinear.*

**2** ◯ 15 ◯ 16 ◯ 17

**3.** Digital video signals can be recorded (18) *only on videotape* (19) *only on a computer disk* (20) *on tape as well as on disk.*

**3** ◯ 18 ◯ 19 ◯ 20

**4.** A high-capacity hard drive can record (21) *only digital information* (22) *only analog information* (23) *both digital and analog information.*

**4** ◯ 21 ◯ 22 ◯ 23

**5.** You can reduce file size with (24) *compression* (25) *larger-capacity hard disks* (26) *larger tape width.*

**5** ◯ 24 ◯ 25 ◯ 26

**6.** The NTSC signal is based on a (27) *composite* (28) *Y/C component* (29) *Y/color difference component* signal.

**6** ◯ 27 ◯ 28 ◯ 29

**7.** An ESS system stores individual frames in (30) *analog* (31) *digital* (32) *digital or analog* form.

**7** ◯ 30 ◯ 31 ◯ 32

**8.** The type of compression that looks for redundancies from one frame to the next is (33) *intraframe* (34) *interframe* (35) *lossless.*

**8** ◯ 33 ◯ 34 ◯ 35

**9.** You can use a ¼-inch mini-cassette for recording (36) *standard digital signals only* (37) *HDV only* (38) *standard digital and HDV signals.*

**9** ◯ 36 ◯ 37 ◯ 38

**10.** DVCPRO and DVCAM camcorders record (39) *analog* (40) *digital* audio and video signals and use (41) *¼-inch* (42) *½-inch* cassettes. **(Fill in two bubbles.)**

**10** ◯ 39 ◯ 40
◯ 41 ◯ 42

SECTION TOTAL

## REVIEW OF VIDEO-RECORDING AND PRODUCTION FACTORS

*Select the correct answers and fill in the bubbles with the corresponding numbers.*

**1.** The video leader  (43) *should*  (44) *should not*  contain a 0 VU audio tone and (45) *should*  (46) *should not*  include the slate. ***(Fill in two bubbles.)***

**1**  ◯ 43   ◯ 44
   ◯ 45   ◯ 46

**2.** Because color bars help the videotape operator match the technical aspects of the playback VTR and the playback monitor, you should record them (47) *at the beginning of the video recording*  (48) *right after the video leader* (49) *at the end of the video recording*  for at least  (50) *10 seconds* (51) *30 seconds*  (52) *5 minutes.* ***(Fill in two bubbles.)***

**2**  ◯ 47   ◯ 48   ◯ 49
   ◯ 50   ◯ 51   ◯ 52

**3.** The field log is normally kept by the  (53) *TD*  (54) *VO*  (55) *VTR operator.*

**3**  ◯ 53   ◯ 54   ◯ 55

**4.** To protect a cassette recording from being accidentally erased, the cassette tab  (56) *must be removed or in the open position*  (57) *must be in place or in the closed position*  (58) *cannot prevent erasure.*

**4**  ◯ 56   ◯ 57   ◯ 58

**5.** Nonlinear editing requires the transfer of relevant source tapes to the computer hard drive  (59) *only of analog tapes*  (60) *only of digital tapes* (61) *of analog and digital tapes.*

**5**  ◯ 59   ◯ 60   ◯ 61

**6.** "Blackening" a tape means to  (62) *record a time code*  (63) *mark the tape box with black letters*  (64) *erase the tape*  so that you can  (65) *identify the tape*  (66) *lay a control track.* ***(Fill in two bubbles.)***

**6**  ◯ 62   ◯ 63   ◯ 64
   ◯ 65   ◯ 66

**7.** The two essential items on a slate are the  (67) *title and take number*  (68) *title and executive producer.*

**7**  ◯ 67   ◯ 68

**SECTION TOTAL** ☐

## REVIEW QUIZ

Mark the following statements as true or false by filling in the bubbles in the
**T** (for true) or **F** (for false) column.

|  |  | T | F |
|---|---|---|---|
| **1.** | NTSC signal and composite signal mean the same thing. | 1 ○ 69 | ○ 70 |
| **2.** | When dubbing videotapes, analog systems produce much more noise in subsequent generations than do digital ones. | 2 ○ 71 | ○ 72 |
| **3.** | In a Y/color difference component system, the Y and R–Y/B–Y signals are kept separate throughout the entire recording process. | 3 ○ 73 | ○ 74 |
| **4.** | The Y/C component system means that the color yellow has been added to the color signals. | 4 ○ 75 | ○ 76 |
| **5.** | You can use videotape to record analog or digital signals. | 5 ○ 77 | ○ 78 |
| **6.** | You can use a hard disk to record analog or digital signals. | 6 ○ 79 | ○ 80 |
| **7.** | In analog recording, each video frame is marked by two spikes (sync pulses). | 7 ○ 81 | ○ 82 |
| **8.** | When a camera feeds a switcher in addition to its own VTR, it is no longer an iso camera. | 8 ○ 83 | ○ 84 |
| **9.** | The video leader includes a 0 VU test tone. | 9 ○ 85 | ○ 86 |
| **10.** | You can use prerecorded color bars for the video leader. | 10 ○ 87 | ○ 88 |

SECTION
TOTAL ☐

## PROBLEM-SOLVING APPLICATIONS

1. Your assistant shows you the first draft of an entry form for a statewide video competition. The specifications for tape formats read as follows: "Only ½-inch or DVCAM formats will be accepted." Will you recommend any changes to these specifications? If so, why? If not, why not?

2. The financial officer of your company tells you that his friend told him to upgrade your camcorders to the DVCPRO format because the cameras are relatively inexpensive and, best of all, you could retain all the old VHS editing equipment. What is your reply? Why?

3. The department head tells you not to bother with nonlinear editing systems because they are so much slower than linear cuts-only systems and, besides, not much more accurate. What is your reply?

4. The TD tells you, the videotape editor, to "bump up" the DVCPRO source tapes if you expect to do extensive postproduction. But the director thinks the DVCPRO tapes can be edited without bumping up. Whose advice should you follow? Why?

5. Design a practical field log format that contains all the essential information.

6. Explain the purpose of each element in a video leader.

# 13 Postproduction Editing

## REVIEW OF KEY TERMS

*Match each term with its appropriate definition by filling in the corresponding bubble.*

1. insert editing
2. nonlinear on-line editing
3. nonlinear editing

4. linear editing
5. nonlinear off-line editing
6. off-line editing

7. assemble editing
8. edit controller
9. EDL
10. window dub

**A.** Consists of edit-in and edit-out points expressed in time code numbers.

**A**  ○ ○ ○ ○ ○
   1   2   3   4   5
   ○ ○ ○ ○ ○
   6   7   8   9   10

**B.** Editing that uses tape-based systems.

**B**  ○ ○ ○ ○ ○
   1   2   3   4   5
   ○ ○ ○ ○ ○
   6   7   8   9   10

**C.** Adding shots on videotape without prior recording of a control track.

**C**  ○ ○ ○ ○ ○
   1   2   3   4   5
   ○ ○ ○ ○ ○
   6   7   8   9   10

**D.** A "bumped-down" copy of all sources with the time code keyed onto each frame.

**D**  ○ ○ ○ ○ ○
   1   2   3   4   5
   ○ ○ ○ ○ ○
   6   7   8   9   10

**E.** Requires the prior laying of a control track.

**E**  ○ ○ ○ ○ ○
   1   2   3   4   5
   ○ ○ ○ ○ ○
   6   7   8   9   10

PAGE TOTAL ☐

| 1. insert editing | 4. linear editing | 7. assemble editing |
|---|---|---|
| 2. nonlinear on-line editing | 5. nonlinear off-line editing | 8. edit controller |
| | | 9. EDL |
| 3. nonlinear editing | 6. off-line editing | 10. window dub |

**F.** Recapturing the shots at a higher resolution.

F  ○ ○ ○ ○ ○
   1  2  3  4  5
   ○ ○ ○ ○ ○
   6  7  8  9  10

**G.** Process that produces the EDL or a videotape not used for broadcast.

G  ○ ○ ○ ○ ○
   1  2  3  4  5
   ○ ○ ○ ○ ○
   6  7  8  9  10

**H.** Capturing video footage at a lower resolution to save storage space and processing time.

H  ○ ○ ○ ○ ○
   1  2  3  4  5
   ○ ○ ○ ○ ○
   6  7  8  9  10

**I.** Device that triggers certain play and editing functions in the source and record VTRs.

I  ○ ○ ○ ○ ○
   1  2  3  4  5
   ○ ○ ○ ○ ○
   6  7  8  9  10

**J.** Allows instant random access to and easy rearrangement of shots from video and audio information stored in digital form.

J  ○ ○ ○ ○ ○
   1  2  3  4  5
   ○ ○ ○ ○ ○
   6  7  8  9  10

PAGE TOTAL [     ]

SECTION TOTAL [     ]

# REVIEW OF EDITING SYSTEMS

*Select the correct answers and fill in the bubbles with the corresponding numbers.*

**1.** The edit controller will  (11) *automatically backspace the source VTR to the exact preroll point, but not the record VTR*  (12) *backspace both VTRs automatically*  (13) *help you backspace manually via the tape counter.*

**1** ○ 11   ○ 12   ○ 13

**2.** In nonlinear editing, capturing refers to  (14) *what the camera recorded on the source tapes*  (15) *dubbing the source tapes to an edit master tape*  (16) *importing digital source material into computer storage.*

**2** ○ 14   ○ 15   ○ 16

**3.** Linear systems  (17) *allow*  (18) *do not allow*  random access to the source material and use  (19) *videotape*  (20) *disk-based*  storage systems. **(Fill in two bubbles.)**

**3** ○ 17   ○ 18
   ○ 19   ○ 20

**4.** Nonlinear systems  (21) *allow*  (22) *do not allow*  random access to the source material and use  (23) *videotape*  (24) *disk-based*  storage systems. **(Fill in two bubbles.)**

**4** ○ 21   ○ 22
   ○ 23   ○ 24

**5.** The operational principle of nonlinear editing is  (25) *copying images from source to record device*  (26) *rearranging audio and video data files*  (27) *transferring digital data from a VTR to a hard drive.*

**5** ○ 25   ○ 26   ○ 27

**6.** The operational principle of linear editing is  (28) *file management*  (29) *transferring data from a VTR to a hard drive*  (30) *copying selected portions of source tapes.*

**6** ○ 28   ○ 29   ○ 30

**7.** Compared with linear editing, nonlinear editing systems require you to pay  (31) *less*  (32) *more*  (33) *the same*  attention to shot continuity in the shooting phase.

**7** ○ 31   ○ 32   ○ 33

**8.** Compared with linear editing, an accurate EDL is  (34) *more*  (35) *less*  (36) *equally*  important in nonlinear editing.

**8** ○ 34   ○ 35   ○ 36

SECTION TOTAL ☐

## REVIEW OF LINEAR EDITING FEATURES AND CONTROLS

*Select the correct answers and fill in the bubbles with the corresponding numbers.*
*Fill in two bubbles for problems 1 through 6.*

1. In the assemble editing mode, the record VTR (37) *will* (38) *will not* copy the control track of the source tape, so you (39) *need* (40) *do not need* to prerecord a continuous control track on the edit master tape.

    **1** ○ ○ ○ ○
       37  38  39  40

2. In the insert editing mode, the record VTR (41) *will* (42) *will not* re-create the control track from the source tape, so you (43) *need* (44) *do not need* to prerecord a continuous control track on the edit master tape.

    **2** ○ ○ ○ ○
       41  42  43  44

3. Insert edits are (45) *more* (46) *less* stable than assemble edits and are (47) *more* (48) *less* likely to cause sync rolls.

    **3** ○ ○ ○ ○
       45  46  47  48

4. When using SMPTE time code, you (49) *can* (50) *cannot* dub it in later over existing source tapes and (51) *must* (52) *must not* necessarily show the actual time during which the production took place.

    **4** ○ ○ ○ ○
       49  50  51  52

5. The control track editing system is (53) *more accurate* (54) *less accurate* in locating a specific frame than the time code system because it (55) *marks* (56) *does not mark* each individual frame with a unique address.

    **5** ○ ○ ○ ○
       53  54  55  56

6. Identify mistakes in the pulse-count display in this figure and fill in the bubbles with the corresponding numbers.

    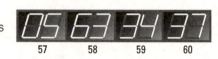

         57       58       59       60

    **6** ○ ○ ○ ○
       57  58  59  60

7. Select the correct pulse-count display that exhibits the actual edit-in point of the edit master tape shown in the following figure and fill in the bubble with the corresponding number.

    **7** ○ ○ ○ ○
       61  62  63  64

**Tape is 15:25 minutes in from start**

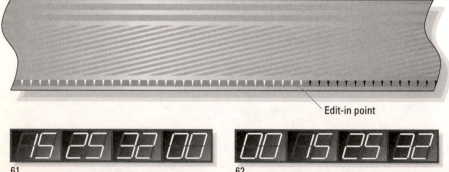

Edit-in point

61     62     63     64

PAGE TOTAL

**8.** To perform split edits (editing video and audio separately), you need to be in the (65) *digital* (66) *insert* (67) *assemble* mode.

**9.** Fill in the bubbles whose numbers correspond with the numbers identifying the correct insert and assemble edits shown in the following figures.

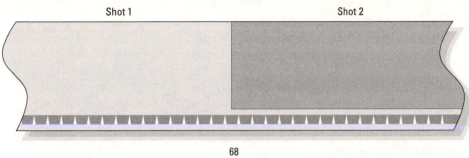

68

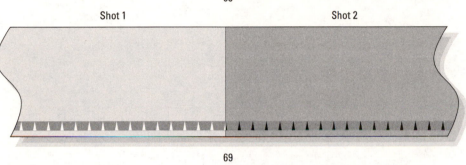

69

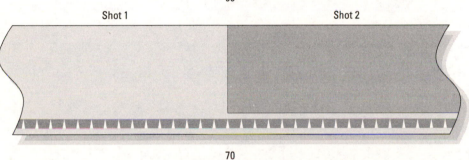

70

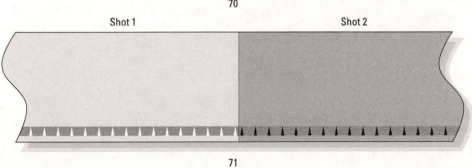

71

**a.** correct insert edit

**b.** correct assemble edit

**10.** To prepare properly for insert editing, you must (72) *prerecord black before using the source tapes* (73) *lay a control track for the edit master tape* (74) *simply record time code during the videotaping of the source material.*

| 10 | ○ 72 | ○ 73 | ○ 74 |

**11.** To prepare properly for assemble editing, you must (75) *lay a continuous control track for the edit master tape* (76) *lay a control track for all source tapes to be used* (77) *do nothing to the tapes you are using.*

| 11 | ○ 75 | ○ 76 | ○ 77 |

PAGE TOTAL

SECTION TOTAL

## REVIEW OF NONLINEAR EDITING FEATURES AND TECHNIQUES

*Select the correct answers and fill in the bubbles with the corresponding numbers.*

1. One of the most common video compression techniques is  (78) *MPEG-2* (79) *MP3*  (80) *NTSC.*

   **1**  ○ 78   ○ 79   ○ 80

2. Videotape instead of a hard disk for nonlinear editing can be used  (81) *only if the video footage is digitized*  (82) *only if the video footage is uncompressed* (83) *not at all.*

   **2**  ○ 81   ○ 82   ○ 83

3. Interframe compression means that  (84) *each frame is individually compressed*  (85) *a group of frames are compressed at the same time* (86) *each frame is compressed in relation to the others.*

   **3**  ○ 84   ○ 85   ○ 86

4. Assuming that a specific EDL contains all basic information, it can be used (87) *only for linear editing*  (88) *only for nonlinear editing*  (89) *for linear and nonlinear editing.*

   **4**  ○ 87   ○ 88   ○ 89

5. With intraframe compression each frame is compressed  (90) *independently* (91) *in relation to the preceding frame*  (92) *in relation to all other frames.*

   **5**  ○ 90   ○ 91   ○ 92

6. In nonlinear editing, capturing requires that all video and audio information is (93) *digitized*  (94) *decompressed*  (95) *compressed.*

   **6**  ○ 93   ○ 94   ○ 95

7. When compared with uncompressed video, lossy compression is preferable because it  (96) *maintains higher-quality video and audio*  (97) *uses less data storage space*  (98) *contains less video noise.*

   **7**  ○ 96   ○ 97   ○ 98

**SECTION TOTAL** [    ]

*Select the correct answers and fill in the bubbles with the corresponding numbers.*

1. You are given a storyboard to assist you in your single-camera EFP of a conversation between a man and a woman (see the following figure). For each storyboard pair, indicate whether the shots (99) *can* (100) *cannot* be edited together, assuming normal continuity-editing principles.

a.
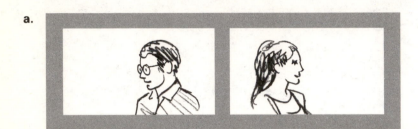

1a   ◯    ◯
    99    100

b.
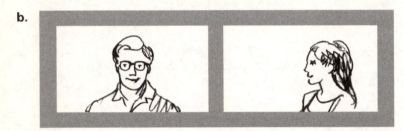

1b   ◯    ◯
    99    100

c.
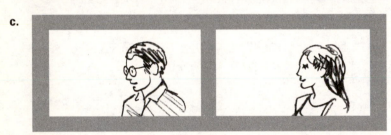

1c   ◯    ◯
    99    100

d.
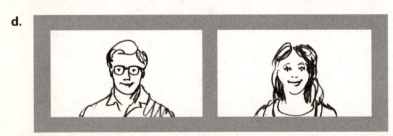

1d   ◯    ◯
    99    100

e.
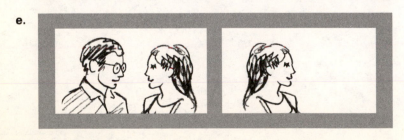

1e   ◯    ◯
    99    100

PAGE TOTAL [    ]

**2.** From the screen images below (repeated on the following page), select the sequence pair you would get when cutting from camera 1 to camera 2 as shown in the diagrams of the camera positions.

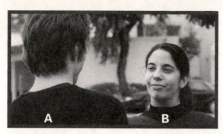

101

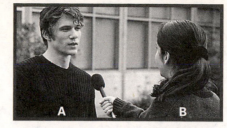

102

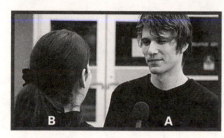

103

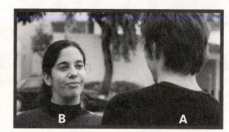

104

**a.** Camera setup A

**2a** ○ ○ ○ ○
101 102 103 104

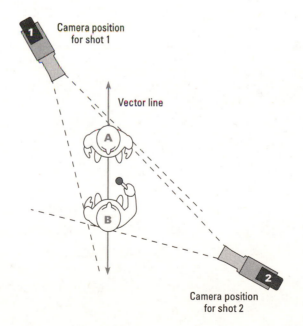

Camera position
for shot 1

Vector line

Camera position
for shot 2

PAGE
TOTAL

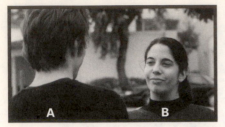

101

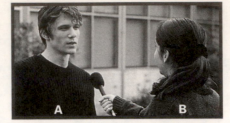

102

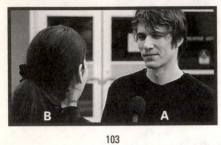

103

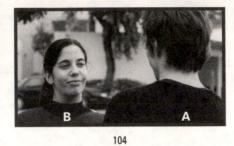

104

**b.** Camera setup B

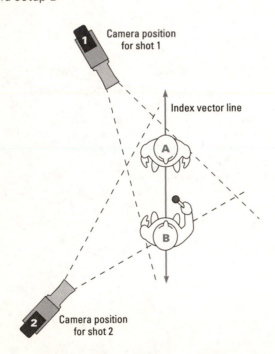

Camera position
for shot 1

Index vector line

Camera position
for shot 2

Course No. _____     Date _____     Name _____

**3.** In the following diagram of a simple interview, select the two cameras that will facilitate optimal cross-shooting and fill in the bubbles with the corresponding numbers.

105

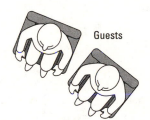
Host          Guests

108

106

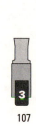
107

**4.** In the following three diagrams, select the camera that is in the *wrong* place for proper continuity editing and fill in the corresponding bubble.

**a.** Cutting from two-shots of piano player and singer to CUs.

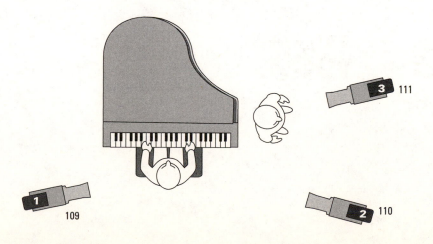
109                                                   111
                                                      110

**3**  ◯ ◯ ◯ ◯
      105 106 107 108

**4a** ◯        ◯        ◯
      109      110      111

P A G E
T O T A L   [          ]

© 2006 Thomson Wadsworth

*Chapter 13 — Postproduction Editing*

**115**

**b.** Cutting from camera 1 to a different point of view of the university president and her husband during a reception.

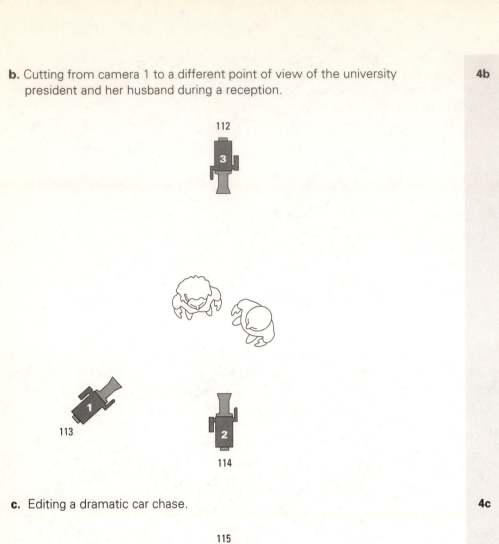

**c.** Editing a dramatic car chase.

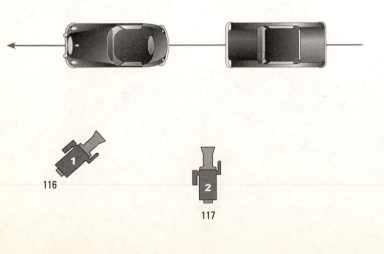

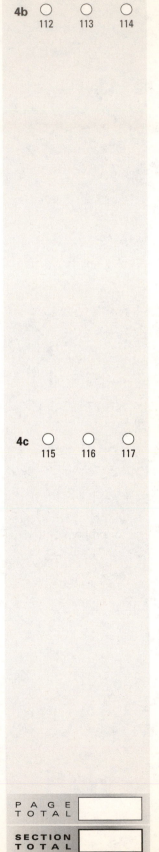

P A G E
T O T A L

S E C T I O N
T O T A L

Course No. _____  Date _____  Name _____

## REVIEW QUIZ

*Mark the following statements as true or false by filling in the bubbles in the*
**T** *(for true) or* **F** *(for false) column.*

|  |  | T | F |
|---|---|---|---|
| **1.** | Nonlinear editing can be done with high-end VTRs. | 1 ○ 118 | ○ 119 |
| **2.** | You should use insert editing only when replacing a shot in an edit master tape. | 2 ○ 120 | ○ 121 |
| **3.** | The concept of AB-roll editing does not apply to nonlinear editing. | 3 ○ 122 | ○ 123 |
| **4.** | Contrary to linear editing, an EDL is not practical in nonlinear editing. | 4 ○ 124 | ○ 125 |
| **5.** | Time code must be recorded during the actual production to achieve a continuous frame address. | 5 ○ 126 | ○ 127 |
| **6.** | The capture of source footage in nonlinear editing requires the prior digitizing of all video and audio information. | 6 ○ 128 | ○ 129 |
| **7.** | MPEG-2 is a lossless compression technique. | 7 ○ 130 | ○ 131 |
| **8.** | In continuity editing, we are concerned primarily with maintaining the mental map. | 8 ○ 132 | ○ 133 |
| **9.** | Ethical considerations are the purview of the director and have no place in the busy editing room. | 9 ○ 134 | ○ 135 |
| **10.** | A VTR log is equally helpful to linear and nonlinear editing. | 10 ○ 136 | ○ 137 |
| **11.** | Vectors indicate the principal directions of lines, motions, or someone pointing within a shot. | 11 ○ 138 | ○ 139 |
| **12.** | Postproduction editing is done primarily to fix production mistakes. | 12 ○ 140 | ○ 141 |
| **13.** | EFP and more-elaborate postproduction editing require the careful logging of all source tapes. | 13 ○ 142 | ○ 143 |
| **14.** | A jump cut may be used effectively in complexity editing. | 14 ○ 144 | ○ 145 |
| **15.** | Interframe compression means the simultaneous compression of several frames. | 15 ○ 146 | ○ 147 |

SECTION TOTAL [ ]

© 2006 Thomson Wadsworth

## PROBLEM-SOLVING APPLICATIONS

1. When editing your EFP material in the assemble mode for a rough-cut, you experience several sync rolls. When you show the rough-cut to the director, he wants to make sure that all transitions are clean. What editing mode would you have to use to ensure "clean transitions"? Explain the features of the selected mode that prevent editing breakups.

2. The novice director warns you, the editor, that the new client is known to change her mind frequently and may require substantive editing changes right in the middle of the show. The director is worried that such major changes may cause serious time delays. Assuming that you are working with a nonlinear editing system, what would you tell the director? Be specific.

3. The same director tells you to be sure to capture the entire source tapes at the highest resolution even for an off-line rough-cut because "once in the computer, you are stuck with what you imported." What is your reaction? Why?

4. Even with your new nonlinear editing system, it is cumbersome to find shots that show the new car model traveling in specific screen directions. The producer suggests that you note the various vectors when logging the source footage. What does she mean? How can doing this help you locate the desired shots?

5. The same producer tells you that even in complexity editing you should never, ever, "cross the line." What does she mean? Do you agree with her?

6. The director is a big fan of nonlinear editing because fixing mistakes in post-production is "now a snap." What is your reaction? Give specific examples.

# 14 Visual Effects

## REVIEW OF KEY TERMS

*Match each term with its appropriate definition by filling in the corresponding bubble.*

1. diffusion filter
2. key
3. chroma key
4. matte key

5. wipe
6. computer-manipulated effect
7. DVE

8. star filter
9. defocus
10. SEG

**A.** Electronically cut-in title whose letters are filled with shades of gray or a specific color.

A  ○ ○ ○ ○ ○
   1  2  3  4  5
  ○ ○ ○ ○ ○
   6  7  8  9  10

**B.** Digital video effect based on an existing image.

B  ○ ○ ○ ○ ○
   1  2  3  4  5
  ○ ○ ○ ○ ○
   6  7  8  9  10

**C.** Cutting in an image (usually lettering) into a background image.

C  ○ ○ ○ ○ ○
   1  2  3  4  5
  ○ ○ ○ ○ ○
   6  7  8  9  10

**D.** Key effect that uses color (usually blue) for the backdrop.

D  ○ ○ ○ ○ ○
   1  2  3  4  5
  ○ ○ ○ ○ ○
   6  7  8  9  10

**E.** Lens attachment that produces a soft image.

E  ○ ○ ○ ○ ○
   1  2  3  4  5
  ○ ○ ○ ○ ○
   6  7  8  9  10

PAGE TOTAL [ ]

| 1. diffusion filter | 5. wipe | 8. star filter |
|---|---|---|
| 2. key | 6. computer-manipulated effect | 9. defocus |
| 3. chroma key | | 10. SEG |
| 4. matte key | 7. DVE | |

**F.** Stands for digital video effects.

F  ○ ○ ○ ○ ○
   1  2  3  4  5
   ○ ○ ○ ○ ○
   6  7  8  9  10

**G.** Transition in which the new image seems to push the old one off the screen.

G  ○ ○ ○ ○ ○
   1  2  3  4  5
   ○ ○ ○ ○ ○
   6  7  8  9  10

**H.** Device that changes prominent light sources into starlike light beams.

H  ○ ○ ○ ○ ○
   1  2  3  4  5
   ○ ○ ○ ○ ○
   6  7  8  9  10

**I.** Lens-activated transitional device to show gradual visual impairment.

I  ○ ○ ○ ○ ○
   1  2  3  4  5
   ○ ○ ○ ○ ○
   6  7  8  9  10

**J.** Produces analog wipe patterns and keys.

J  ○ ○ ○ ○ ○
   1  2  3  4  5
   ○ ○ ○ ○ ○
   6  7  8  9  10

PAGE TOTAL

SECTION TOTAL

*Chapter 14 — Visual Effects*

## REVIEW OF STANDARD ELECTRONIC EFFECTS

**1.** Fill in the bubbles whose numbers correspond with the appropriate key effects shown in the following figures.

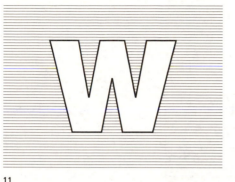

11

12

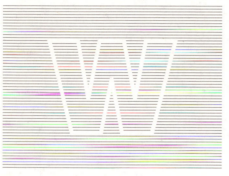

13

14

    **a.** matte key

    **b.** outline mode

    **c.** drop-shadow mode

    **d.** edge mode

**1a**  ◯ ◯ ◯ ◯
    11  12  13  14

**1b**  ◯ ◯ ◯ ◯
    11  12  13  14

**1c**  ◯ ◯ ◯ ◯
    11  12  13  14

**1d**  ◯ ◯ ◯ ◯
    11  12  13  14

PAGE
TOTAL

**2.** Fill in the bubbles whose numbers correspond with the appropriate electronic effects illustrated in the following figures.

15
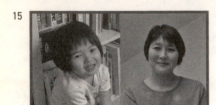

16
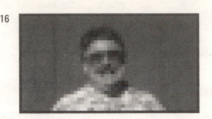

17
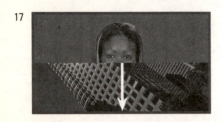

18
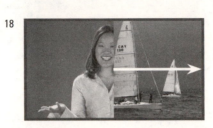

19
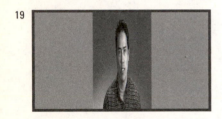

20
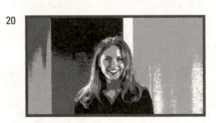

21
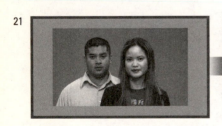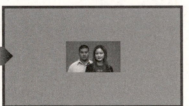

22
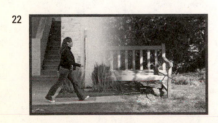

23
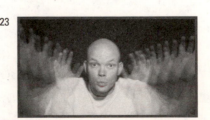

**a.** shrinking

2a ○ ○ ○ ○ ○
   15  16  17  18  19
   ○ ○ ○ ○
   20  21  22  23

**b.** echo effect

2b ○ ○ ○ ○ ○
   15  16  17  18  19
   ○ ○ ○ ○
   20  21  22  23

**c.** soft wipe

2c ○ ○ ○ ○ ○
   15  16  17  18  19
   ○ ○ ○ ○
   20  21  22  23

**d.** vertical stretching

2d ○ ○ ○ ○ ○
   15  16  17  18  19
   ○ ○ ○ ○
   20  21  22  23

**e.** vertical wipe

2e ○ ○ ○ ○ ○
   15  16  17  18  19
   ○ ○ ○ ○
   20  21  22  23

**f.** mosaic

2f ○ ○ ○ ○ ○
   15  16  17  18  19
   ○ ○ ○ ○
   20  21  22  23

**g.** posterization

2g ○ ○ ○ ○ ○
   15  16  17  18  19
   ○ ○ ○ ○
   20  21  22  23

**h.** split screen

2h ○ ○ ○ ○ ○
   15  16  17  18  19
   ○ ○ ○ ○
   20  21  22  23

**i.** horizontal wipe

2i ○ ○ ○ ○ ○
   15  16  17  18  19
   ○ ○ ○ ○
   20  21  22  23

PAGE TOTAL [ ]

**3.** Fill in the bubbles whose numbers correspond with the button you would have to press on the pattern selector to create the various effects illustrated in the following figures.

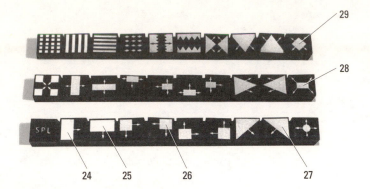

**a.**

**b.**

PAGE TOTAL [        ]

c.

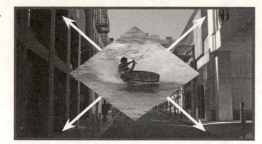

3c  ○ 24    ○ 25    ○ 26
    ○ 27    ○ 28    ○ 29

d.

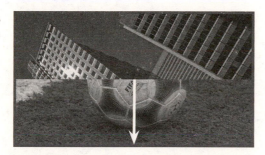

3d  ○ 24    ○ 25    ○ 26
    ○ 27    ○ 28    ○ 29

e.

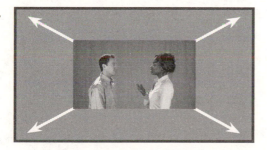

3e  ○ 24    ○ 25    ○ 26
    ○ 27    ○ 28    ○ 29

f.

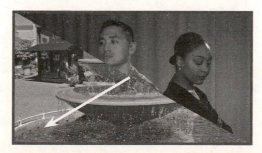

3f  ○ 24    ○ 25    ○ 26
    ○ 27    ○ 28    ○ 29

PAGE
TOTAL [ ]

***Chapter 14*** — *Visual Effects*

*Select the correct answers and fill in the bubbles with the corresponding numbers.*

**4.** The two most frequently used backdrop colors for studio chroma-key effects are (30) *yellow and blue* (31) *blue and red* (32) *green and blue.*

**5.** To de-emphasize the demarcation line in a split-screen effect, we use (33) *a quad-split* (34) *compression* (35) *a soft wipe.*

**6.** To create echo, stretching, and compression effects, you need (36) *DVE* (37) *an SEG* (38) *a TBC.*

**7.** A secondary frame (screen within a screen) (39) *can have a vertical aspect ratio* (40) *must have a 4 × 3 horizontal aspect ratio* (41) *must have a 16 × 9 HDTV aspect ratio.*

**8.** Shrinking effects differ from box wipes because (42) *they maintain the total picture and aspect ratio during the reduction* (43) *the reduction can get smaller than a box wipe* (44) *they need a blue background.*

**9.** During posterization (45) *the brightness values are reduced* (46) *the saturation is reversed* (47) *all brightness values are reversed.*

**10.** A fly effect shows (48) *a computer-generated fly buzzing through the picture* (49) *the B video zooming from zero to a certain image size and spinning into a specific A video screen location* (50) *the B image moving along the z-axis and appearing to fly through the screen into off-screen space.*

## REVIEW QUIZ

*Mark the following statements as true or false by filling in the bubbles in the*
*__T__ (for true) or __F__ (for false) column.*

|   |   | T | F |
|---|---|---|---|
| **1.** | To achieve the cube rotation or cube-spin effect, you need first to videotape the actual spin of a cube and then fill the sides with images. | **1** ○ 51 | ○ 52 |
| **2.** | Electronically cutting out portions of a background image and filling them with color is called a superimposition. | **2** ○ 53 | ○ 54 |
| **3.** | A drop shadow makes lettering look three-dimensional. | **3** ○ 55 | ○ 56 |
| **4.** | With DVE you can change the size and the aspect ratio of an insert without losing any portion of the inserted image. | **4** ○ 57 | ○ 58 |
| **5.** | You can accomplish a wipe effect with analog equipment. | **5** ○ 59 | ○ 60 |
| **6.** | When chroma keying, the object that is to be keyed into the background must be blue. | **6** ○ 61 | ○ 62 |
| **7.** | In a mosaic effect, you can change the size of the tiles (image squares) electronically. | **7** ○ 63 | ○ 64 |
| **8.** | You can achieve a split-screen effect simply by stopping a horizontal wipe midway. | **8** ○ 65 | ○ 66 |
| **9.** | The box wipe is identical to the shrinking effect. | **9** ○ 67 | ○ 68 |
| **10.** | You need DVE equipment to continuously change the size of a circle wipe. | **10** ○ 69 | ○ 70 |

SECTION TOTAL ☐

## PROBLEM-SOLVING APPLICATIONS

1. When checking the chroma key of a weathercaster standing in front of a weather map, you, the TD, discover that the key is not "clean." The talent's dark hair seems to have a blue and purple halo, and the outline of her head and shoulders is not sharp against the weather map. Assuming that the problem does not lie with the chroma-key equipment, what is the problem? What, if anything, can you do to minimize or eliminate it?

2. The preview monitor shows that the outline-mode title key is hard to read over the busy background. How could you, the TD, make the title more readable without changing the font or the background?

3. When you, the TD, preview the key of a C.G. title, the white letters tear at the edges. How can you correct this problem?

4. The AD informs you, the director, that a dancer, who is supposed to be chroma-keyed over a videotaped landscape scene, wears a saturated medium-blue leotard. The AD is very concerned about this, but the TD assures you that he has already taken care of the problem. What was the potential problem? What did the TD do to solve it?

5. The director asks you, the TD, to start out with a full-screen image of the opening news story and then shrink the entire scene and place it over the newscaster's shoulder. The switcher is equipped with an SEG but not with DVE. What is your response? Why?

# 15 Design

## REVIEW OF KEY TERMS

*Match each term with its appropriate definition by filling in the corresponding bubble.*

1. aspect ratio
2. flat
3. C.G.
4. floor plan

5. essential area
6. scanning area
7. props

8. floor plan pattern
9. color compatibility
10. grayscale

**A.** The section of the television picture, centered within the scanning area, that the home viewer sees.

A  ◯ ◯ ◯ ◯ ◯
   1  2  3  4  5
   ◯ ◯ ◯ ◯ ◯
   6  7  8  9  10

**B.** The width-to-height proportions of the television screen.

B  ◯ ◯ ◯ ◯ ◯
   1  2  3  4  5
   ◯ ◯ ◯ ◯ ◯
   6  7  8  9  10

**C.** Colors with enough brightness contrast for good monochrome reproduction.

C  ◯ ◯ ◯ ◯ ◯
   1  2  3  4  5
   ◯ ◯ ◯ ◯ ◯
   6  7  8  9  10

**D.** Furniture and other objects used for set decorations or by actors or performers.

D  ◯ ◯ ◯ ◯ ◯
   1  2  3  4  5
   ◯ ◯ ◯ ◯ ◯
   6  7  8  9  10

**E.** The picture area usually seen on the camera viewfinder and the preview monitor.

E  ◯ ◯ ◯ ◯ ◯
   1  2  3  4  5
   ◯ ◯ ◯ ◯ ◯
   6  7  8  9  10

PAGE TOTAL [      ]

| 1. aspect ratio | 5. essential area | 8. floor plan pattern |
| 2. flat | 6. scanning area | 9. color compatibility |
| 3. C.G. | 7. props | 10. grayscale |
| 4. floor plan | | |

**F.** A dedicated computer that electronically produces letters, numbers, and simple graphic images for video display.

F  ○ ○ ○ ○ ○
   1  2  3  4  5
   ○ ○ ○ ○ ○
   6  7  8  9  10

**G.** A diagram of scenery and major set properties drawn on a grid.

G  ○ ○ ○ ○ ○
   1  2  3  4  5
   ○ ○ ○ ○ ○
   6  7  8  9  10

**H.** A piece of standing scenery used as a background or to simulate a wall.

H  ○ ○ ○ ○ ○
   1  2  3  4  5
   ○ ○ ○ ○ ○
   6  7  8  9  10

**I.** A spectrum showing the intermediate steps from TV white to TV black.

I  ○ ○ ○ ○ ○
   1  2  3  4  5
   ○ ○ ○ ○ ○
   6  7  8  9  10

**J.** A plan of the studio floor with the grid but without a set design.

J  ○ ○ ○ ○ ○
   1  2  3  4  5
   ○ ○ ○ ○ ○
   6  7  8  9  10

PAGE TOTAL [ ]

SECTION TOTAL [ ]

*Chapter 15 — Design*

Course No. _____  Date _____  Name _____

## REVIEW OF TELEVISION GRAPHICS

*Select the correct answers and fill in the bubbles with the corresponding numbers.*

**1.** On a normal grayscale (nine-step or seven-step), *1* represents (11) *TV white* (12) *TV black* (13) *100% reflectance.*

**1** ○ 11  ○ 12  ○ 13

**2.** The aesthetic energy of a color is principally determined by (14) *hue and brightness* (15) *the color itself* (16) *saturation and brightness.*

**2** ○ 14  ○ 15  ○ 16

**3.** All lettering must be contained within the (17) *scanning area* (18) *screen area* (19) *essential area.*

**3** ○ 17  ○ 18  ○ 19

**4.** The standard television aspect ratio is (20) *4 × 3* (21) *8 × 12* (22) *16 × 9.* For HDTV it is (23) *4 × 3* (24) *8 × 12* (25) *16 × 9.* **(Fill in two bubbles.)**

**4** ○ 20  ○ 21  ○ 22
   ○ 23  ○ 24  ○ 25

**5.** Color compatibility refers to using colors that differ distinctly as to (26) *hue* (27) *saturation* (28) *brightness.*

**5** ○ 26  ○ 27  ○ 28

**6.** Dead zones are (29) *uninteresting picture areas* (30) *the empty vertical bars when showing standard TV on HDTV* (31) *a sound problem in studio areas.*

**6** ○ 29  ○ 30  ○ 31

**7.** Normally, low-energy colors are used more for the (32) *foreground* (33) *middleground* (34) *background* in a scene.

**7** ○ 32  ○ 33  ○ 34

**8.** To store a great many video frames for instant access, you need (35) *an ESS system* (36) *DVE* (37) *an SEG.*

**8** ○ 35  ○ 36  ○ 37

**9.** The whiteboard writing shown in the photo below is (38) *appropriate* (39) *inappropriate* because it (40) *is within the scanning area* (41) *does not permit good CUs.* **(Fill in two bubbles.)**

**9** ○ 38  ○ 39
   ○ 40  ○ 41

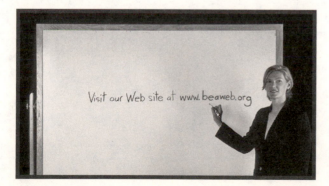

PAGE TOTAL [ ]

**10.** The vertically oriented chart in this diagram is  (42) *acceptable*  (43) *not acceptable* for shooting with a studio camera because  (44) *it is not in proper aspect ratio*  (45) *the camera can tilt in a close-up.* **(Fill in two bubbles.)**

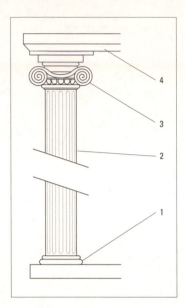

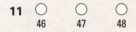

**11.** The edge distortion as shown in this figure is called  (46) *antialiasing*  (47) *aliasing*  (48) *pixel distortion.*

# BECA

**12.** Fill in the bubbles whose numbers correspond with the appropriate title areas in the figure.

**a.** total graphic screen area

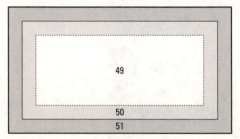

**b.** essential area

**c.** scanning area

**13.** Fill in the bubbles whose numbers correspond with the appropriate aspect ratio or frame adjustments in the figure.

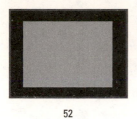
52

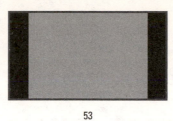
53

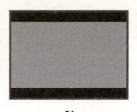
54

**a.** letterboxing

|13a| ◯ 52 | ◯ 53 | ◯ 54 |

**b.** pillarboxing

|13b| ◯ 52 | ◯ 53 | ◯ 54 |

**c.** frame adjustment

|13c| ◯ 52 | ◯ 53 | ◯ 54 |

**14.** Fill in the bubbles whose numbers correspond with the type of distortion that results from adjusting one aspect ratio to fit another.

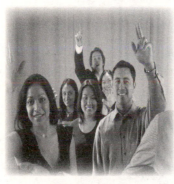
55

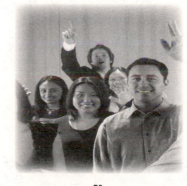
56

**a.** a 16 × 9 shot viewed full-screen on a 4 × 3 monitor

|14a| ◯ 55 | ◯ 56 |

**b.** a 4 × 3 shot viewed full-screen on a 16 × 9 monitor

|14b| ◯ 55 | ◯ 56 |

PAGE TOTAL [ ]

**15.** The following six figures show various television graphics displayed on well-adjusted preview monitors. These monitors show the entire scanning area. For each figure state whether you would (57) *accept* (58) *not accept* the television graphic because it has (59) *inappropriate style* (60) *enough contrast between figure and ground* (61) *scattered information* (62) *good grouping of words* (63) *letters that are too small* (64) *information that lies outside the essential area* (65) *letters that get lost in the busy background.* **(Fill in the two bubbles that seem most appropriate for each graphic.)**

Design by
Gary Palmatier

a.

*Nuclear Crisis*

b.

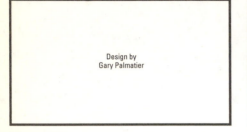

Zoom control ring

Focus ring        Iris control ring

c.

EARTHQUAKE

d.

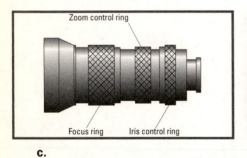

Crew
Susan Walters        Robaire Ream
Cathy Linberg        Karen Austin
Deirdre Cavanaugh
Elizabeth von Radics
Ryan E. Vesely        Susan Gall
Ken Baird        Dory Schaeffer
Stacey Purviance

e.

**Dancers:**
**Stephanie Ream**
**Nicole Beynon**
**Florence Holsted**
**Jane Frost**

f.

15a  ○ 57    ○ 58
○ 59   ○ 60   ○ 61   ○ 62
○ 63   ○ 64   ○ 65

15b  ○ 57    ○ 58
○ 59   ○ 60   ○ 61   ○ 62
○ 63   ○ 64   ○ 65

15c  ○ 57    ○ 58
○ 59   ○ 60   ○ 61   ○ 62
○ 63   ○ 64   ○ 65

15d  ○ 57    ○ 58
○ 59   ○ 60   ○ 61   ○ 62
○ 63   ○ 64   ○ 65

15e  ○ 57    ○ 58
○ 59   ○ 60   ○ 61   ○ 62
○ 63   ○ 64   ○ 65

15f  ○ 57    ○ 58
○ 59   ○ 60   ○ 61   ○ 62
○ 63   ○ 64   ○ 65

PAGE TOTAL

SECTION TOTAL

## REVIEW OF SCENERY AND SCENIC DESIGN

**1.** Fill in the bubbles whose numbers correspond with the numbers identifying the various set pieces shown below.

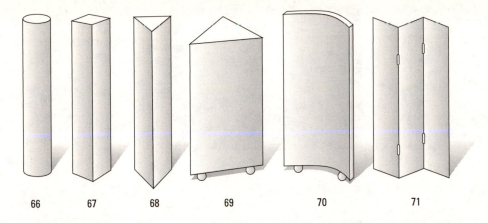

66    67    68    69    70    71

**a.** pylon

**b.** screen

**c.** round pillar

**d.** square pillar

**e.** sweep

**f.** periaktos

| | | | |
|---|---|---|---|
| **1a** | ○ 66 | ○ 67 | ○ 68 |
| | ○ 69 | ○ 70 | ○ 71 |
| **1b** | ○ 66 | ○ 67 | ○ 68 |
| | ○ 69 | ○ 70 | ○ 71 |
| **1c** | ○ 66 | ○ 67 | ○ 68 |
| | ○ 69 | ○ 70 | ○ 71 |
| **1d** | ○ 66 | ○ 67 | ○ 68 |
| | ○ 69 | ○ 70 | ○ 71 |
| **1e** | ○ 66 | ○ 67 | ○ 68 |
| | ○ 69 | ○ 70 | ○ 71 |
| **1f** | ○ 66 | ○ 67 | ○ 68 |
| | ○ 69 | ○ 70 | ○ 71 |

P A G E
T O T A L

2. For the simple sets shown below, select the floor plan shown on the facing page that most closely corresponds and fill in the appropriate bubbles.
*(Assume that the camera shoots straight-on. Note that there are floor plans that do not match any of the set photos. The floor plans are not to scale.)*

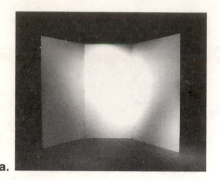

a.

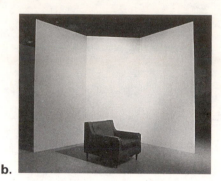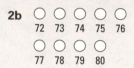

b.

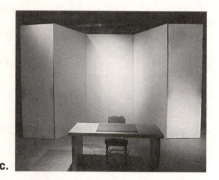

c.

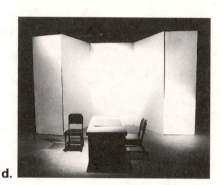

d.

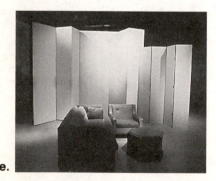

e.

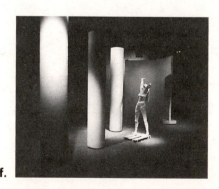

f.

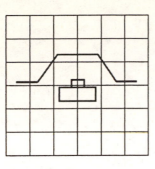

72

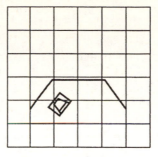

73

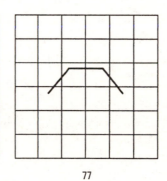

74

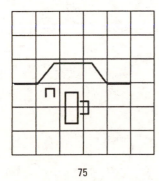

75

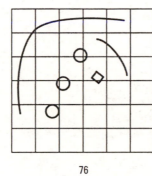

76

77

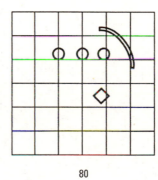

78

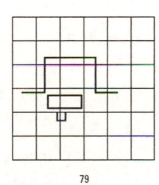

79

80

*Select the correct answers and fill in the bubbles with the corresponding numbers.*

3. To elevate scenery, properties, or action areas, we use (81) *periaktoi* (82) *platforms* (83) *pylons.*

    **3**   ◯ 81   ◯ 82   ◯ 83

4. The usual height for standard set units is (84) *7 feet* (85) *10 feet* (86) *14 feet.* For studios with low ceilings, it is (87) *6 feet* (88) *8 feet* (89) *12 feet.* **(Fill in two bubbles.)**

    **4**   ◯ 84   ◯ 85   ◯ 86   ◯ 87   ◯ 88   ◯ 89

5. Pictures and draperies are (90) *set dressings* (91) *set decorations* (92) *hand props.*

    **5**   ◯ 90   ◯ 91   ◯ 92

6. The standard backgrounds to simulate interior and exterior walls are called (93) *cycs* (94) *flats* (95) *drops.*

    **6**   ◯ 93   ◯ 94   ◯ 95

7. The continuous piece of canvas or muslin along two, three, or even all four studio walls to form a uniform background is referred to as (96) *a drop* (97) *canvas backing* (98) *a cyclorama.*

    **7**   ◯ 96   ◯ 97   ◯ 98

PAGE TOTAL ☐

SECTION TOTAL ☐

## REVIEW QUIZ

*Mark the following statements as true or false by filling in the bubbles in the* **T** *(for true) or* **F** *(for false) column.*

|   |   | T | F |
|---|---|---|---|

1. The scanning area is contained within the essential area.

   **1** ○ 99   ○ 100

2. There is an inevitable picture loss when wide-screen movies are shown in their true aspect ratio on a traditional (4 x 3) television screen.

   **2** ○ 101   ○ 102

3. A black drape makes an ideal chroma-key backdrop.

   **3** ○ 103   ○ 104

4. A periaktos looks like a large pylon.

   **4** ○ 105   ○ 106

5. The energy of a color is determined primarily by hue.

   **5** ○ 107   ○ 108

6. Distinctly different hues (such as red and green) guarantee good brightness contrast.

   **6** ○ 109   ○ 110

7. For normal screen titles, all written information must extend beyond the scanning area.

   **7** ○ 111   ○ 112

8. A floor plan must show the location of flats but can omit the set properties.

   **8** ○ 113   ○ 114

9. A good floor plan will aid the LD in the lighting design.

   **9** ○ 115   ○ 116

10. Hardwall scenery is preferred for permanent sets.

    **10** ○ 117   ○ 118

11. Pillarboxing is used to fit a 4 × 3 aspect ratio into a 16 × 9 screen without distortion.

    **11** ○ 119   ○ 120

12. The proper arrangement of multiple screen elements can prevent screen clutter.

    **12** ○ 121   ○ 122

SECTION TOTAL ☐

# PROBLEM-SOLVING APPLICATIONS

1. You are asked to direct a variety of shows and evaluate the location sketch or floor plans (see a through c). Please be specific as to the potential problems in scale (sets and props), camera accessibility and acceptable shots, lighting, and talent traffic.

   a. Here is a floor plan for a two-camera live-on-tape production of a panel discussion by six prominent businesspeople and a moderator.

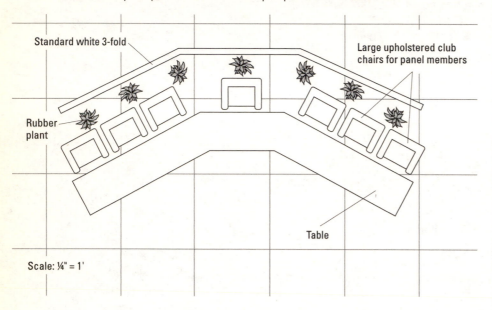

Standard white 3-fold

Large upholstered club chairs for panel members

Rubber plant

Table

Scale: ¼" = 1'

   b. This floor plan is for a two-camera live interview set for a morning show.

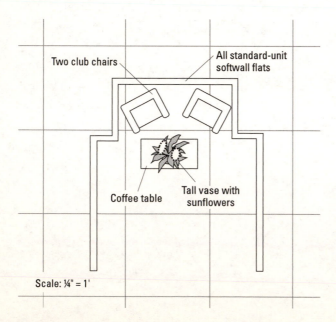

Two club chairs

All standard-unit softwall flats

Coffee table

Tall vase with sunflowers

Scale: ¼" = 1'

**c.** This location sketch shows the office of the CEO, who would like to make her monthly 11 a.m. live-satellite TV report from behind her desk.

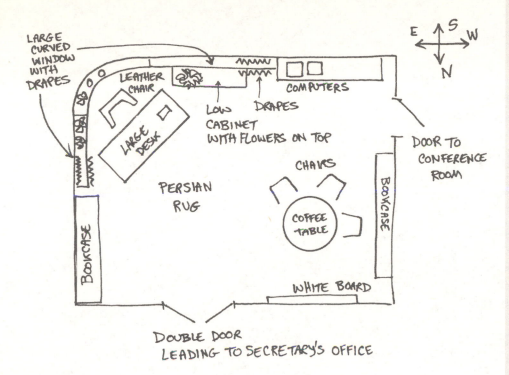

2. Draw a floor plan for a weekly interview show dealing with the art and media scene in your city. The host will interview guests from stage, screen, and radio. Include a detailed prop list. (Use one of the floor plan patterns provided at the back of this book.)

3. Draw a floor plan for a morning news set. The anchors are a woman and a man, and the news content is geared more toward local gossip than international politics. (Use one of the floor plan patterns provided at the back of this book.)

4. The general manager of your corporation would like you to use a highly detailed photo of the latest computer design as the background for the opening and closing titles. Can you accommodate the request and still make the titles optimally readable?

5. The art director proudly shows you the dancing Chinese-like lettering he has created with his titling software for the name identification of the new Chinese consul. Would you use such a title key? If so, why? If not, why not?

# 16 Production People

---

## REVIEW OF KEY TERMS

*Match each term with its appropriate definition by filling in the corresponding bubble.*

1. actor
2. talent
3. performer

4. cue card
5. below-the-line personnel

6. blocking
7. above-the-line personnel

**A.** Technical production people who normally operate the production equipment.

A  ○ ○ ○ ○
   1  2  3  4
   ○ ○ ○
   5  6  7

**B.** Nontechnical production people who are occupied primarily with nontechnical matters, such as producing or writing.

B  ○ ○ ○ ○
   1  2  3  4
   ○ ○ ○
   5  6  7

**C.** A person who appears on-camera in a nondramatic role.

C  ○ ○ ○ ○
   1  2  3  4
   ○ ○ ○
   5  6  7

**D.** A person who appears on-camera in a dramatic role.

D  ○ ○ ○ ○
   1  2  3  4
   ○ ○ ○
   5  6  7

PAGE
TOTAL [    ]

| 1. actor | 4. cue card | 6. blocking |
|---|---|---|
| 2. talent | 5. below-the-line personnel | 7. above-the-line personnel |
| 3. performer | | |

**E.** A large, hand-lettered card that contains on-air copy.

E  ○ ○ ○ ○
   1 2 3 4
   ○ ○ ○
   5 6 7

**F.** All people who regularly appear on television.

F  ○ ○ ○ ○
   1 2 3 4
   ○ ○ ○
   5 6 7

**G.** Carefully worked-out movement and actions by the talent.

G  ○ ○ ○ ○
   1 2 3 4
   ○ ○ ○
   5 6 7

PAGE TOTAL [　　]

SECTION TOTAL [　　]

## REVIEW OF PRODUCTION PERSONNEL

**1.** Match each job title with its appropriate definition by filling in the corresponding bubble.

| | | |
|---|---|---|
| (8) floor manager | (12) director | (16) C.G. operator |
| (9) videotape operator | (13) art director | (17) VO |
| (10) audio technician | (14) TD | (18) DP |
| (11) executive producer | (15) producer | (19) PA |

**a.** Relays director's cues to talent.

**1a**
○ ○ ○ ○
8　9　10　11
○ ○ ○ ○
12　13　14　15
○ ○ ○ ○
16　17　18　19

**b.** Responsible for transforming a script into effective video and audio images.

**1b**
○ ○ ○ ○
8　9　10　11
○ ○ ○ ○
12　13　14　15
○ ○ ○ ○
16　17　18　19

**c.** Does the switching and usually acts as technical crew chief.

**1c**
○ ○ ○ ○
8　9　10　11
○ ○ ○ ○
12　13　14　15
○ ○ ○ ○
16　17　18　19

**d.** Assists the producer and/or director during a production.

**1d**
○ ○ ○ ○
8　9　10　11
○ ○ ○ ○
12　13　14　15
○ ○ ○ ○
16　17　18　19

**e.** In charge of one or several program series; manages budget, among other things, and coordinates with station management, advertising agencies, networks, and financial supporters.

**1e**
○ ○ ○ ○
8　9　10　11
○ ○ ○ ○
12　13　14　15
○ ○ ○ ○
16　17　18　19

PAGE TOTAL ☐

| (8) floor manager | (12) director | (16) C.G. operator |
|---|---|---|
| (9) videotape operator | (13) art director | (17) VO |
| (10) audio technician | (14) TD | (18) DP |
| (11) executive producer | (15) producer | (19) PA |

**f.** In charge of videotaping.

**1f**
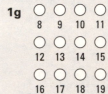

**g.** In charge of an individual production.

**1g**
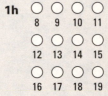

**h.** Works the audio console during a show.

**1h**
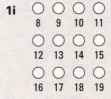

**i.** Types and/or recalls from the computer the names and other graphic material to be integrated with the video image.

**1i**
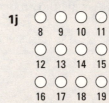

**j.** In EFP, operates the camera and does the lighting.

**1j**

| | | | |
|---|---|---|---|
| ○ 8 | ○ 9 | ○ 10 | ○ 11 |
| ○ 12 | ○ 13 | ○ 14 | ○ 15 |
| ○ 16 | ○ 17 | ○ 18 | ○ 19 |

| P A G E TOTAL | |
|---|---|

| | | |
|---|---|---|
| (8) floor manager | (12) director | (16) C.G. operator |
| (9) videotape operator | (13) art director | (17) VO |
| (10) audio technician | (14) TD | (18) DP |
| (11) executive producer | (15) producer | (19) PA |

**k.** Adjusts camera controls at the CCU for optimal camera pictures.

**1k**
○ ○ ○ ○
8   9  10  11
○ ○ ○ ○
12  13  14  15
○ ○ ○ ○
16  17  18  19

**l.** Responsible for the creative design aspects of a show.

**1l**
○ ○ ○ ○
8   9  10  11
○ ○ ○ ○
12  13  14  15
○ ○ ○ ○
16  17  18  19

PAGE TOTAL [ ]

2. Match each title of news personnel with its appropriate definition by filling in the corresponding bubble.

(20) anchor          (23) news producer        (26) videographer/
(21) sportscaster    (24) assignment editor          shooter
(22) news director   (25) reporter             (27) writer

**a.** Principal presenter of newscast, normally from a studio set.

2a ○ ○ ○ ○
   20 21 22 23
   ○ ○ ○ ○
   24 25 26 27

**b.** On-camera talent, giving sports content.

2b ○ ○ ○ ○
   20 21 22 23
   ○ ○ ○ ○
   24 25 26 27

**c.** Gathers the news stories and often reports on-camera from the field.

2c ○ ○ ○ ○
   20 21 22 23
   ○ ○ ○ ○
   24 25 26 27

**d.** Prepares on-the-air copy for the anchorpersons.

2d ○ ○ ○ ○
   20 21 22 23
   ○ ○ ○ ○
   24 25 26 27

**e.** Responsible for individual news stories for on-the-air use.

2e ○ ○ ○ ○
   20 21 22 23
   ○ ○ ○ ○
   24 25 26 27

**f.** Sends reporters and videographers to specific events.

2f ○ ○ ○ ○
   20 21 22 23
   ○ ○ ○ ○
   24 25 26 27

**g.** Operates camcorder and, in the absence of a reporter, decides what part of the event to cover.

2g ○ ○ ○ ○
   20 21 22 23
   ○ ○ ○ ○
   24 25 26 27

**h.** Responsible for all of the news operations.

2h ○ ○ ○ ○
   20 21 22 23
   ○ ○ ○ ○
   24 25 26 27

PAGE TOTAL ☐

SECTION TOTAL ☐

Course No. _____    Date _____    Name _____

## REVIEW OF PERSONNEL RESPONSIBILITIES

*Identify the production person mainly responsible for the following production activities and fill in the corresponding bubbles.*

1. Two days before the weekly interview show, the senator canceled her guest appearance. The responsibility for finding a replacement rests with the (28) *AD* (29) *producer* (30) *director*.

   1  ○28  ○29  ○30

2. The novice news anchor would like to have the basic cues demonstrated. The cues should be demonstrated on the studio floor by the (31) *floor manager* (32) *TD* (33) *director*.

   2  ○31  ○32  ○33

3. As the director, you want somebody to write down all major and minor problems that show up during rehearsal. For this job you would most likely ask the (34) *floor manager* (35) *producer* (36) *PA*.

   3  ○34  ○35  ○36

4. Two of the three studio cameras produce colors with a distinctly red tinge. To get all three cameras to match with optimal colors, you need to contact the (37) *technical director* (38) *VO* (39) *camera operator*.

   4  ○37  ○38  ○39

5. To increase the overall light level in a scene, you should ask the (40) *PA* (41) *LD* (42) *floor manager*.

   5  ○40  ○41  ○42

6. For your live telecast of the New Year's Day parade, you need someone to type, recall, or change the titles that identify the various floats. For this job you call upon the (43) *graphic artist* (44) *PA* (45) *C.G. operator*.

   6  ○43  ○44  ○45

7. For the upcoming interview with a prominent lawyer, the program director would like to have a lawyer's office set built. He requests the preliminary sketches and the floor plan from the (46) *floor manager* (47) *director* (48) *art director*.

   7  ○46  ○47  ○48

8. To put up and dress the new lawyer's set is the responsibility of the (49) *art director* (50) *floor manager* (51) *PA*.

   8  ○49  ○50  ○51

9. In the absence of a properties manager, all props are usually handled by the (52) *floor manager* (53) *art director* (54) *AD*.

   9  ○52  ○53  ○54

10. Sending a calibration tone to the VTR to match the console output and the VTR input is the job of the (55) *TD* (56) *VTR operator* (57) *audio technician*.

    10  ○55  ○56  ○57

SECTION TOTAL [____]

© 2006 Thomson Wadsworth

**1.** The following pictures show various *time* cues given to the talent by the floor manager. From the list below, select the specific cue illustrated and fill in the bubble with the corresponding number.

(58) standby          (62) stretch          (65) 5 minutes left
(59) cue              (63) wind up          (66) 30 seconds left
(60) speed up         (64) cut              (67) 15 seconds left
(61) on time

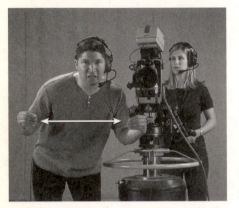

a.                                                b.

**1a** ○ ○ ○ ○ ○
      58 59 60 61 62
      ○ ○ ○ ○ ○
      63 64 65 66 67

**1b** ○ ○ ○ ○ ○
      58 59 60 61 62
      ○ ○ ○ ○ ○
      63 64 65 66 67

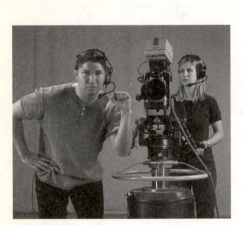

c.                                                d.

**1c** ○ ○ ○ ○ ○
      58 59 60 61 62
      ○ ○ ○ ○ ○
      63 64 65 66 67

**1d** ○ ○ ○ ○ ○
      58 59 60 61 62
      ○ ○ ○ ○ ○
      63 64 65 66 67

PAGE
TOTAL [      ]

Course No. _____   Date _____   Name _____

| (58) standby | (62) stretch | (65) 5 minutes left |
| (59) cue | (63) wind up | (66) 30 seconds left |
| (60) speed up | (64) cut | (67) 15 seconds left |
| (61) on time | | |

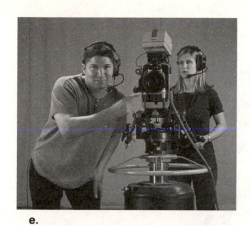

e.

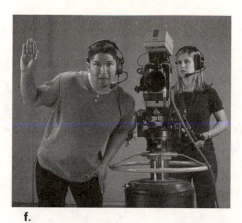

f.

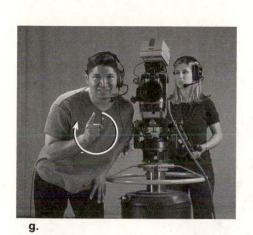

g.

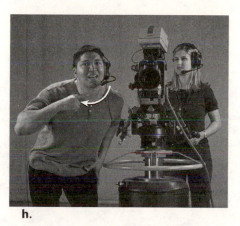

h.

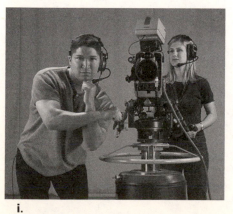

i.

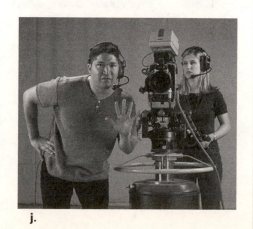

j.

1e  ○ ○ ○ ○ ○
    58 59 60 61 62
    ○ ○ ○ ○ ○
    63 64 65 66 67

1f  ○ ○ ○ ○ ○
    58 59 60 61 62
    ○ ○ ○ ○ ○
    63 64 65 66 67

1g  ○ ○ ○ ○ ○
    58 59 60 61 62
    ○ ○ ○ ○ ○
    63 64 65 66 67

1h  ○ ○ ○ ○ ○
    58 59 60 61 62
    ○ ○ ○ ○ ○
    63 64 65 66 67

1i  ○ ○ ○ ○ ○
    58 59 60 61 62
    ○ ○ ○ ○ ○
    63 64 65 66 67

1j  ○ ○ ○ ○ ○
    58 59 60 61 62
    ○ ○ ○ ○ ○
    63 64 65 66 67

PAGE TOTAL ☐

© 2006 Thomson Wadsworth

*Chapter 16* — *Production People*

**151**

**2.** The following pictures show various *directional* and *audio* cues given to the talent by the floor manager. From the list below, select the specific cue illustrated and fill in the bubble with the corresponding number.

(68) closer      (71) OK      (74) closer to mic

(69) step back      (72) speak up      (75) keep talking

(70) walk      (73) tone down

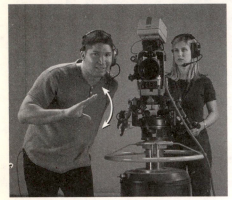

a.

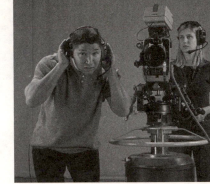

b.

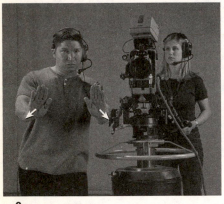

c.

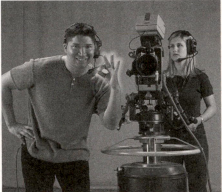

d.

**2a** ◯ ◯ ◯ ◯
   68   69   70   71
   ◯ ◯ ◯ ◯
   72   73   74   75

**2b** ◯ ◯ ◯ ◯
   68   69   70   71
   ◯ ◯ ◯ ◯
   72   73   74   75

**2c** ◯ ◯ ◯ ◯
   68   69   70   71
   ◯ ◯ ◯ ◯
   72   73   74   75

**2d** ◯ ◯ ◯ ◯
   68   69   70   71
   ◯ ◯ ◯ ◯
   72   73   74   75

PAGE TOTAL ☐

| (68) closer | (71) OK | (74) closer to mic |
| (69) step back | (72) speak up | (75) keep talking |
| (70) walk | (73) tone down | |

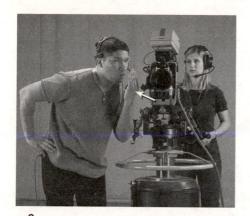

e.

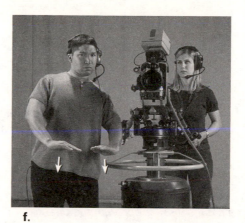

f.

**2e** ○ ○ ○ ○
68 69 70 71
○ ○ ○ ○
72 73 74 75

**2f** ○ ○ ○ ○
68 69 70 71
○ ○ ○ ○
72 73 74 75

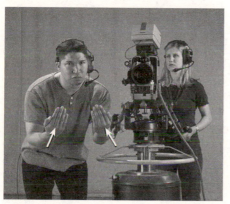

g.

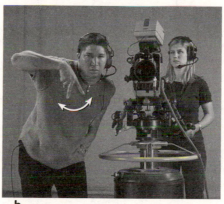

h.

**2g** ○ ○ ○ ○
68 69 70 71
○ ○ ○ ○
72 73 74 75

**2h** ○ ○ ○ ○
68 69 70 71
○ ○ ○ ○
72 73 74 75

PAGE
TOTAL

*Select the correct answers and fill in the bubbles with the corresponding numbers.*

**3.** When demonstrating a product during a two-camera live show, you should orient the product toward the (76) *long-shot camera* (77) *close-up camera* and keep looking at the (78) *long-shot camera* (79) *close-up camera*. **(Fill in two bubbles.)**

**3**  ○ 76  ○ 77
   ○ 78  ○ 79

**4.** When wearing a lavaliere mic, you should (80) *maintain your voice level regardless of how far the camera is away from you* (81) *increase your volume when the camera gets farther away from you* (82) *speak more softly when the camera is relatively close to you.*

**4**  ○ 80  ○ 81  ○ 82

**5.** For the talent the most accurate indicator of the camera's field of view is the (83) *relative distance between talent and camera* (84) *floor manager's cues* (85) *studio monitor.*

**5**  ○ 83  ○ 84  ○ 85

**6.** When you receive cues during the actual videotaping that differ from the rehearsed ones, you should (86) *execute the action as rehearsed* (87) *promptly follow the floor manager's cues* (88) *check with the director.*

**6**  ○ 86  ○ 87  ○ 88

**7.** When demonstrating a small object, you should (89) *hold it as close to the lens as possible* (90) *keep it as steady as possible on the display table* (91) *lift it up for optimal camera pickup.*

**7**  ○ 89  ○ 90  ○ 91

**8.** From the list below, select the microphone most appropriate for the various performance and acting tasks and fill in the bubbles with the corresponding numbers.

(92) lavaliere        (95) fishpole mic        (98) wireless hand mic
(93) boom mic         (96) stand mic           (99) wireless lavaliere
(94) hand mic         (97) desk mic

**a.** Interview with a celebrity at a busy airport gate

**8a** ○ 92  ○ 93  ○ 94  ○ 95
    ○ 96  ○ 97  ○ 98  ○ 99

**b.** News anchors who remain seated throughout a studio newscast

**8b** ○ 92  ○ 93  ○ 94  ○ 95
    ○ 96  ○ 97  ○ 98  ○ 99

**c.** Moderating a panel discussion with six people

**8c** ○ 92  ○ 93  ○ 94  ○ 95
    ○ 96  ○ 97  ○ 98  ○ 99

PAGE TOTAL [     ]

| | | |
|---|---|---|
| (92) lavaliere | (95) fishpole mic | (98) wireless hand mic |
| (93) boom mic | (96) stand mic | (99) wireless lavaliere |
| (94) hand mic | (97) desk mic | |

**d.** Singer who is also dancing, accompanied by a large band

**8d**
○ ○ ○ ○
92 93 94 95
○ ○ ○ ○
96 97 98 99

**e.** Lead guitarist with a rock band, who also sings and talks to the audience

**8e**
○ ○ ○ ○
92 93 94 95
○ ○ ○ ○
96 97 98 99

**f.** Two actors doing an outdoor scene

**8f**
○ ○ ○ ○
92 93 94 95
○ ○ ○ ○
96 97 98 99

**g.** Multiple-camera scene in a soap opera, involving three actors

**8g**
○ ○ ○ ○
92 93 94 95
○ ○ ○ ○
96 97 98 99

**h.** Sounds of breathing and skis on snow during a downhill race

**8h**
○ ○ ○ ○
92 93 94 95
○ ○ ○ ○
96 97 98 99

**9.** When you notice that you're looking into the wrong (not switched on-the-air) camera, you should (100) *look down and then up again into the on-the-air camera* (101) *glance immediately over to the on-the-air camera* (102) *keep looking into the wrong camera until it is punched up on the air.*

**9**
○ ○ ○
100 101 102

**10.** When asked for an audio level, you should (103) *quickly count to ten* (104) *say one sentence with a slightly lower voice than when on the air* (105) *speak with your on-the-air voice until told that the level has been taken.*

**10**
○ ○ ○
103 104 105

PAGE TOTAL [ ]

SECTION TOTAL [ ]

## REVIEW OF ACTING TECHNIQUES

*Select the correct answers and fill in the bubbles with the corresponding numbers.*

1. When blocked in the camera-far position in an O/S shot, you must make sure that you see the  (106) *key light*  (107) *floor manager*  (108) *camera lens.*

   **1**  ○ 106   ○ 107   ○ 108

2. The television camera looks at you primarily in  (109) *long shots*  (110) *close-ups*  (111) *low-level shots.*

   **2**  ○ 109   ○ 110   ○ 111

3. Television plays are videotaped  (112) *in the order of scenes from the beginning to the end of the script*  (113) *in brief scenes, grouped by settings, characters involved, and so forth*  (114) *according to the mood of the director.*

   **3**  ○ 112   ○ 113   ○ 114

4. When on a close-up, you should  (115) *slow down*  (116) *accelerate* (117) *change the rehearsed blocking of*  your actions.

   **4**  ○ 115   ○ 116   ○ 117

5. A "blocking map" is  (118) *a rough map drawn by the floor manager* (119) *a mental map to remember prominent positions*  (120) *the lines drawn on the floor by the AD.*

   **5**  ○ 118   ○ 119   ○ 120

6. When auditioning for a television drama, you should  (121) *apply your theatre technique to show that you have stage training*  (122) *wear something unusual so the director will remember you*  (123) *internalize the role as much as possible.*

   **6**  ○ 121   ○ 122   ○ 123

7. When acting for television, you should project your motions and emotions as you would on the stage  (124) *every time the camera is relatively far away* (125) *never*  (126) *when there is a prolonged dialogue pause.*

   **7**  ○ 124   ○ 125   ○ 126

   *See also the blocking exercise (#6) in the Problem-solving Applications on page 159.*

SECTION TOTAL [     ]

Course No. _____ Date _____ Name _____

## REVIEW OF MAKEUP AND CLOTHING

*Select the correct answers and fill in the bubbles with the corresponding numbers.*

1. Under high-color-temperature lighting, use (127) *warm* (128) *cool* (129) *neutral* makeup colors.

   **1** ◯ ◯ ◯
      127 128 129

2. When applying makeup the ideal lighting conditions are the same as or close to those of (130) *your customary dressing room* (131) *the actual production environment* (132) *normal 3,200K studio lights.*

   **2** ◯ ◯ ◯
      130 131 132

3. You can counteract a heavy five-o'clock shadow by applying a light layer of (133) *bluish* (134) *skin-colored* (135) *yellow* greasepaint.

   **3** ◯ ◯ ◯
      133 134 135

4. One of the most widely used makeup foundations is (136) *pancake* (137) *grease base* (138) *pan stick.*

   **4** ◯ ◯ ◯
      136 137 138

5. When working with prosumer or consumer cameras under low-light conditions, you should avoid wearing (139) *red* (140) *green* (141) *blue* foundation.

   **5** ◯ ◯ ◯
      139 140 141

6. As a weathercaster you can wear blue so long as the chroma-key backdrop is (142) *blue* (143) *green* (144) *white.*

   **6** ◯ ◯ ◯
      142 143 144

7. The dress of a pop singer has many rhinestones that sparkle under the colored stage lights. This dress is (145) *acceptable* (146) *not acceptable* because (147) *the color camera can handle small areas of bright light* (148) *there is too much brightness contrast* (149) *it will cause moiré patterns* (150) *it will help raise the baselight level.* **(Fill in two bubbles.)**

   **7** ◯ ◯
      145 146
   ◯ ◯ ◯ ◯
   147 148 149 150

8. Clothing with thin, highly contrasting stripes or checkered patterns is (151) *acceptable* (152) *not acceptable* because (153) *the camera CCD can handle such a contrast* (154) *it provides exciting patterns* (155) *it causes moiré color vibrations* (156) *it is too detailed for the camera to see.* **(Fill in two bubbles.)**

   **8** ◯ ◯
      151 152
   ◯ ◯ ◯ ◯
   153 154 155 156

**SECTION TOTAL** ☐

Mark the following statements as true or false by filling in the bubbles in the *T* (for true) or *F* (for false) column.

| | | T | F |
|---|---|---|---|
| **1.** | In multicamera productions, the TD is normally doing the switching. | **1** ○ 157 | ○ 158 |
| **2.** | The line producer normally negotiates with the budgets of a show series. | **2** ○ 159 | ○ 160 |
| **3.** | All ENG operations are supervised by the technical supervisor. | **3** ○ 161 | ○ 162 |
| **4.** | In the studio the camera operators normally do the talent cueing. | **4** ○ 163 | ○ 164 |
| **5.** | The art director draws the floor plan and recommends the type of set properties. | **5** ○ 165 | ○ 166 |
| **6.** | The audio technician works the audio console during a show. | **6** ○ 167 | ○ 168 |
| **7.** | The floor manager is principally responsible for the budget. | **7** ○ 169 | ○ 170 |
| **8.** | The assignment editor tells reporters and videographers where to go and what to cover. | **8** ○ 171 | ○ 172 |
| **9.** | The news director directs the live newscast from the studio control room. | **9** ○ 173 | ○ 174 |
| **10.** | The principal function of master control is to tell everyone where the event to be televised is taking place. | **10** ○ 175 | ○ 176 |
| **11.** | Writers are usually considered above-the-line production personnel. | **11** ○ 177 | ○ 178 |
| **12.** | Television actors always portray someone else. | **12** ○ 179 | ○ 180 |
| **13.** | When you are on the air in a dramatic role, you must follow the rehearsed blocking precisely. | **13** ○ 181 | ○ 182 |
| **14.** | When you work with a teleprompter, it is best to move the camera as close to the talent as possible. | **14** ○ 183 | ○ 184 |
| **15.** | What you wear when auditioning for a role is unimportant. | **15** ○ 185 | ○ 186 |

**SECTION TOTAL** [ ]

## PROBLEM-SOLVING APPLICATIONS

1. The camera operators for a weekly two-camera interview series tell you, the producer, that they do not need a director because the studio setup does not change and they have done the show many times and know every shot by heart. Do you agree? If so, why? If not, why not?

2. The manager of a corporation tells you that she has agreed to pay specific fees for the above-the-line personnel but a lump sum for all below-the-line costs. What does she mean?

3. The VO tells you, the director, that it is the LD's responsibility to white-balance the cameras by providing adequate light for the camera. What is your response?

4. The producer insists on having a chair between the TD and the director during the live telecast of a parade so that she can override the director's commands and call for certain camera shots that "have more visual impact." Would you support this arrangement? If so, why? If not, why not?

5. The ENG camera operator suggests that you, the reporter, do your stand-up report in front of the bright, sunlit wall of city hall. According to the camera operator, the automatic iris control would guarantee the high-key lighting effect which, in turn, would reflect the upbeat story you have to tell. Do you agree with the camera operator? If so, why? If not, why not? What is your response?

6. To practice blocking, write down a series of moves that carry you around your kitchen. For example, you can start at the stove, then get the teakettle out of the cupboard, fill it with water, and put it on the stove, go back to pick up the telephone, put down the telephone to answer the door, and so forth. Try to hit the same marks each time you go through the routine. If possible, have a friend videotape your blocking maneuvers from the same camera position. You can then compare the tapes and check how accurate your blocking was. As part of the same exercise, you can use various props (kitchen utensils) to see how the camera's field of view (LS to ECU) will influence your handling of them.

7. Pretend that you, person A, are receiving a telephone call from person B. In this scene we see and hear only person A (you). Using exactly the same dialogue (see the script on the following page), adapt your delivery and acting style to at least two of the following circumstances:

   a. B calls to tell you that he/she has just got an exciting new job.

   b. B calls to tell you that he/she has just lost his/her job.

   c. B has just had an accident with your new car.

   d. B has broken the engagement.

   e. B has won first prize in a video competition.

   Locate the scene anywhere you like. You may do well to write the other part of the phone conversation so that you can "listen" to the virtual B part of the dialogue and respond more convincingly.

PHONE CONVERSATION

**PERSON A**

Hello?

Hi.

Fine, and you?

Good.

No.

No, really. It's always good to hear from you.

I beg your pardon?

You must be kidding.

Yes.

No.

What does Alex say to all this?

No. Should I?

I don't know.

Perhaps.

You want me to come over now?

Yes. Really.

Well, this changes things somewhat.

I think so.

I'm not so sure.

Yes. No. I . . .

All right. But not . . .

OK.

If you think this is . . .

Definitely.

Good-bye . . . When?

No. Really.

Good-bye.

# 17 Producing

## ▌ REVIEW OF KEY TERMS

*Match each term with its appropriate definition by filling in the corresponding bubble.*

1. psychographics
2. effect-to-cause model
3. medium requirements
4. facilities request

5. process message
6. target audience
7. demographics
8. treatment

9. share
10. rating
11. time line
12. production schedule

**A.** All content and production elements needed to generate the process message.

A
○ ○ ○ ○
1 2 3 4
○ ○ ○ ○
5 6 7 8
○ ○ ○ ○
9 10 11 12

**B.** Brief narrative description of a television program.

B
○ ○ ○ ○
1 2 3 4
○ ○ ○ ○
5 6 7 8
○ ○ ○ ○
9 10 11 12

**C.** A list that contains all technical and location equipment needed for a specific production.

C
○ ○ ○ ○
1 2 3 4
○ ○ ○ ○
5 6 7 8
○ ○ ○ ○
9 10 11 12

**D.** The message that the television viewer actually receives.

D
○ ○ ○ ○
1 2 3 4
○ ○ ○ ○
5 6 7 8
○ ○ ○ ○
9 10 11 12

PAGE TOTAL ☐

© 2006 Thomson Wadsworth

| | | | |
|---|---|---|---|
| 1. psychographics | 5. process message | 9. share | |
| 2. effect-to-cause model | 6. target audience | 10. rating | |
| 3. medium requirements | 7. demographics | 11. time line | |
| 4. facilities request | 8. treatment | 12. production schedule | |

**E.** Schedule for activities on the production day.

E
○ ○ ○ ○
1　2　3　4
○ ○ ○ ○
5　6　7　8
○ ○ ○ ○
9　10　11　12

**F.** Audience research factors concerned with such items as consumer buying habits and lifestyles.

F
○ ○ ○ ○
1　2　3　4
○ ○ ○ ○
5　6　7　8
○ ○ ○ ○
9　10　11　12

**G.** The viewer group desired to receive a specific message.

G
○ ○ ○ ○
1　2　3　4
○ ○ ○ ○
5　6　7　8
○ ○ ○ ○
9　10　11　12

**H.** Dates that show preproduction, production, and postproduction activities and deadlines.

H
○ ○ ○ ○
1　2　3　4
○ ○ ○ ○
5　6　7　8
○ ○ ○ ○
9　10　11　12

**I.** The percentage of television households tuned to a specific station in relation to all households with their television sets turned on.

I
○ ○ ○ ○
1　2　3　4
○ ○ ○ ○
5　6　7　8
○ ○ ○ ○
9　10　11　12

PAGE
TOTAL ☐

1.  psychographics
2.  effect-to-cause model
3.  medium requirements
4.  facilities request
5.  process message
6.  target audience
7.  demographics
8.  treatment
9.  share
10. rating
11. time line
12. production schedule

**J.** A production approach, or system, that moves from the idea to the desired effect on the audience.

J  ○ ○ ○ ○
   1 2 3 4
   ○ ○ ○ ○
   5 6 7 8
   ○ ○ ○ ○
   9 10 11 12

**K.** Audience research factors concerned with such items as income and age.

K  ○ ○ ○ ○
   1 2 3 4
   ○ ○ ○ ○
   5 6 7 8
   ○ ○ ○ ○
   9 10 11 12

**L.** Percentage of television households tuned to a specific station in relation to the total number of television households.

L  ○ ○ ○ ○
   1 2 3 4
   ○ ○ ○ ○
   5 6 7 8
   ○ ○ ○ ○
   9 10 11 12

PAGE TOTAL [     ]

SECTION TOTAL [     ]

## REVIEW OF EFFECT-TO-CAUSE MODEL

*Select the correct answers and fill in the bubbles with the corresponding numbers.*

**1.** Identify each part of the effect-to-cause diagram below and fill in the bubbles with the corresponding numbers.

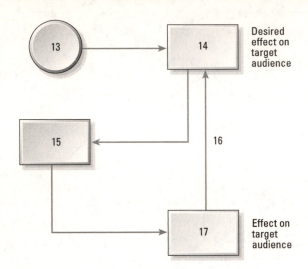

**a.** defined process message

1a  ○ ○ ○ ○ ○
    13  14  15  16  17

**b.** actual process message

1b  ○ ○ ○ ○ ○
    13  14  15  16  17

**c.** initial idea

1c  ○ ○ ○ ○ ○
    13  14  15  16  17

**d.** program content, people, and production elements

1d  ○ ○ ○ ○ ○
    13  14  15  16  17

**e.** feedback

1e  ○ ○ ○ ○ ○
    13  14  15  16  17

PAGE TOTAL

2. In the effect-to-cause model, we move from (18) *idea to medium requirements to production* (19) *idea to production to process message* (20) *idea to process message to medium requirements.*

       2  ◯    ◯    ◯
          18    19    20

3. The most important initial step in the effect-to-cause approach is (21) *determining the available production equipment* (22) *defining the process message* (23) *determining the medium requirements.*

       3  ◯    ◯    ◯
          21    22    23

4. Feedback helps determine (24) *whether the production was efficient* (25) *how close the actual effect came to the process message* (26) *how close the actual effect came to the original idea.*

       4  ◯    ◯    ◯
          24    25    26

5. The medium requirements include (27) *equipment but not people* (28) *equipment and people.*

       5  ◯    ◯
          27    28

6. Medium requirements are basically determined by the (29) *process message* (30) *chief engineer* (31) *available equipment.*

       6  ◯    ◯    ◯
          29    30    31

PAGE TOTAL [ ]

SECTION TOTAL [ ]

# REVIEW OF PRODUCTION METHODS

*Select the correct answers and fill in the bubbles with the corresponding numbers.*

**1.** A show treatment usually contains (32) *a brief narrative description of what we see and hear* (33) *a script sample with major visualization cues* (34) *a one-page sample of the dialogue and the video and audio cues.*

**2.** A good description of the target audience should include (35) *only demographic indicators* (36) *only psychographic indicators* (37) *both demographic and psychographic indicators.*

**3.** A well-stated process message should (38) *include the specific objective of the show* (39) *state the steps of moving from idea to finished show* (40) *describe the process of moving from idea to detailed script.*

**4.** In a large production, the daily activities are supervised by the (41) *line producer* (42) *executive producer* (43) *PA.*

**5.** When preparing a budget, you need to list initially (44) *only the above-the-line items* (45) *only the below-the-line items* (46) *above- and below-the-line and all other production items.*

**6.** Detailed preproduction is necessary for (47) *every production except ENG* (48) *studio productions only* (49) *EFP.*

**7.** When you work for a television station, your show will be listed in the daily log by the (50) *traffic department* (51) *production manager* (52) *program manager.*

**8.** Facilities requests are necessary (53) *only if you are planning a new production* (54) *for every production except ENG* (55) *for the preproduction conference.*

**9.** In the production schedule on the facing page, identify potential problems for each EFP shoot. From the list below, select the items that best describe the problems and fill in the corresponding bubbles. Most shoots have more than one problem. **(Multiple answers are possible.)**

(56) different talent; break in continuity

(57) different director and crew; potential break in style and continuity

(58) need for remote truck questionable relative to the production scope

(59) shooting time too late; will cause lighting and continuity problems in postproduction

(60) should be done in conjunction with similar previous activity or opening

(61) facilities request very late

(62) facilities request too late

(63) too little time allotted

(64) too much time allotted

| | | | |
|---|---|---|---|
| 1 | ○ 32 | ○ 33 | ○ 34 |
| 2 | ○ 35 | ○ 36 | ○ 37 |
| 3 | ○ 38 | ○ 39 | ○ 40 |
| 4 | ○ 41 | ○ 42 | ○ 43 |
| 5 | ○ 44 | ○ 45 | ○ 46 |
| 6 | ○ 47 | ○ 48 | ○ 49 |
| 7 | ○ 50 | ○ 51 | ○ 52 |
| 8 | ○ 53 | ○ 54 | ○ 55 |

PAGE TOTAL ☐

| Show/Scene/Subject | Date/Time | Location | Facilities | Talent/Personnel |
|---|---|---|---|---|
| Leisure City SHOOT 1 OPENING | Aug. 8 8:30 am 4:30 pm | In front of completed model home— Simple opening remarks. 1:00 min. | Normal EFP as per fac. req. Aug. 8 | Talent: LYNNE Director: B.R. Crew A scheduled |
| Leisure City SHOOT 2 | Aug. 9 12:30 pm 1:00 pm | Homes under construction. Show homes being constructed. | Special remote Truck. See equipment fac. req. Aug. 8 | Talent: LYNNE Director: B.R. Crew A scheduled |
| Leisure City SHOOT 3 | Aug. 10 8:30 am 9:00 am | Interior of model home. Shows how Typical home looks and works inside. | Normal EFP as per fac. req. Aug. 7 | Talent: LYNNE Director: B.R. Crew A scheduled |
| Leisure City SHOOT 4 | Aug. 11 7:30 pm 10:30 pm | Homes under construction. | Normal EFP as per fac. req. Aug. 11 | Talent: SUSAN Director: JOHN HEWITT Crew B scheduled |
| Leisure City SHOOT 5 | Aug. 12 8:00 pm 8:30 pm | In front of completed model home— Simple closing remarks. 1:30 min. | Special remote Truck. See equipment fac. req. Aug. 8 | Talent: SUSAN Director: B.R. Crew A scheduled |

**a.** shoot 1

**9a** 56 57 58 59 / 60 61 62 63 64

**b.** shoot 2

**9b** 56 57 58 59 / 60 61 62 63 64

**c.** shoot 3

**9c** 56 57 58 59 / 60 61 62 63 64

**d.** shoot 4

**9d** 56 57 58 59 / 60 61 62 63 64

**e.** shoot 5

**9e** 56 57 58 59 / 60 61 62 63 64

PAGE TOTAL [ ]

SECTION TOTAL [ ]

## REVIEW OF UNIONS AND LEGAL MATTERS

*Select the correct answers and fill in the bubbles with the corresponding numbers.*

1. The theater department of the local high school would like to play its video production of Arthur Miller's *Death of a Salesman* on a local TV station. The student actors (65) *will* (66) *will not* need AFTRA clearance.

   **1** ◯  ◯
       65  66

2. A potential sponsor would like a treatment of the proposed play of your humanities series. Sending the script instead is (67) *acceptable* (68) *not acceptable*.

   **2** ◯  ◯
       67  68

3. For each of the trade unions listed, mark whether it is a (69) *technical* or a (70) *nontechnical* union by filling in the appropriate bubble.

   a. AFM

   **3a** ◯  ◯
       69  70

   b. AFTRA

   **3b** ◯  ◯
       69  70

   c. DGA

   **3c** ◯  ◯
       69  70

   d. IATSE

   **3d** ◯  ◯
       69  70

   e. IBEW

   **3e** ◯  ◯
       69  70

   f. NABET

   **3f** ◯  ◯
       69  70

   g. WGA

   **3g** ◯  ◯
       69  70

   h. SAG

   **3h** ◯  ◯
       69  70

   i. SEG

   **3i** ◯  ◯
       69  70

PAGE TOTAL ☐

4. Determine whether each of the production cases below (71) *requires* or
   (72) *does not require* copyright clearance and fill in the appropriate bubble.

   a. Having your pianist friend play and record her own composition for use as a
      theme on your weekly music series.

      **4a**  ○ 71    ○ 72

   b. Using a recent CD recording of Bach's Toccata and Fugue in F Major as the
      theme for a show on architecture.

      **4b**  ○ 71    ○ 72

   c. Using a Beatles song as the theme for a historical documentary.

      **4c**  ○ 71    ○ 72

   d. Using an art book to make a digital scan of a church floor plan for your
      show on Baroque art.

      **4d**  ○ 71    ○ 72

   e. Using a record album cover as the background for your opening and closing
      titles on a music series.

      **4e**  ○ 71    ○ 72

   f. Using a sixteenth-century book to make a digital scan of a church floor plan
      for your Renaissance show.

      **4f**  ○ 71    ○ 72

   g. Using three different scenes of published plays as the basis for your
      series about acting for the video camera.

      **4g**  ○ 71    ○ 72

   h. Taking close-ups of paintings in your news coverage of the local outdoor
      art festival.

      **4h**  ○ 71    ○ 72

| P A G E TOTAL | |
|---|---|
| **SECTION TOTAL** | |

# REVIEW OF RATINGS

*Select the correct answers and fill in the bubbles with the corresponding numbers.*

1. Share figures are usually (73) *higher* (74) *lower* than rating figures.

   1  ○ 73   ○ 74

2. A rating of 13 indicates that (75) *13 of 2,000* (76) *800 of 6,000* (77) *13 of 1,300* (78) *total television households* (79) *of all households using television* are tuned to your station. **(Fill in two bubbles.)**

   2  ○ 75   ○ 76   ○ 77
      ○ 78   ○ 79

3. A share of 22 means that (80) *175 of 2,200* (81) *22 of 2,200* (82) *175 of 800* (83) *total television households* (84) *of all households using television* are tuned to your station. **(Fill in two bubbles.)**

   3  ○ 80   ○ 81   ○ 82
      ○ 83   ○ 84

4. All rating services use (85) *audience samples* (86) *total populations* as a basis for their figures.

   4  ○ 85   ○ 86

5. HUT is a factor in figuring (87) *shares* (88) *ratings*.

   5  ○ 87   ○ 88

SECTION
TOTAL [ ]

## REVIEW QUIZ

*Mark the following statements as true or false by filling in the bubbles in the* **T** *(for true) or* **F** *(for false) column.*

|   |   | T | F |
|---|---|---|---|
| **1.** | The effect-to-cause model goes from idea to production to audience effect. | **1** ○ 89 | ○ 90 |
| **2.** | Budgets must include expenses for preproduction, production, and all postproduction activities as well as personnel. | **2** ○ 91 | ○ 92 |
| **3.** | The actual process message is the interaction between the television viewer and the audio and visual stimuli of the program. | **3** ○ 93 | ○ 94 |
| **4.** | CDs sold in record stores are in the public domain, so you can use them for television productions without securing copyright clearance. | **4** ○ 95 | ○ 96 |
| **5.** | Broadcast unions include technical personnel only. | **5** ○ 97 | ○ 98 |
| **6.** | The producer works only with nontechnical personnel. | **6** ○ 99 | ○ 100 |
| **7.** | Demographic descriptors help define the target audience. | **7** ○ 101 | ○ 102 |
| **8.** | A show treatment is necessary only for television documentaries. | **8** ○ 103 | ○ 104 |
| **9.** | Because production is primarily a creative activity, any type of production system would prove counterproductive. | **9** ○ 105 | ○ 106 |
| **10.** | Above-the-line budgets deal mostly with technical personnel and equipment costs. | **10** ○ 107 | ○ 108 |
| **11.** | The line producer is responsible primarily for budgets. | **11** ○ 109 | ○ 110 |
| **12.** | The facilities request for a specific production should contain equipment and technical facilities. | **12** ○ 111 | ○ 112 |
| **13.** | Whereas the budget is essential for a program proposal, a description of the target audience is not. | **13** ○ 113 | ○ 114 |
| **14.** | A time line and a production schedule are the same thing. | **14** ○ 115 | ○ 116 |
| **15.** | A good process message should include a clear statement of the desired effect on the target audience. | **15** ○ 117 | ○ 118 |

SECTION TOTAL [    ]

## PROBLEM-SOLVING APPLICATIONS

1. The art director asks you, the producer, whether her floor plan will allow optimal camera traffic. Are you the right person to answer this question? If so, why? If not, who would be the appropriate person to answer this question?

2. Your new comedy series is shot multicamera-style in the studio. You intend to videotape the dress rehearsal and the uninterrupted live-on-tape show for later on-air scheduling. The production manager suggests that you prepare a budget and reserve the facilities for a considerable amount of off- and on-line postproduction editing. Do you agree with the production manager? If so, why? If not, why not?

3. Write an effective program proposal for one or more of the following ideas. The proposal should include these points: (1) program title, (2) target audience, (3) process message (objective), (4) show treatment, (5) ideal broadcast or other distribution channel and time, and (6) tentative budget.

   A series of shows about the effects of television on children

   A weekly fashion show

   A ten-week series on how to preserve water

   A three-show series on your favorite sport

   A five-show series for seventh- and eighth-graders on the dangers of drugs

   A ten-part series about human dignity and happiness

   A ten-part minidoc series on road rage and safe driving

   A ten-part series on the life and work of a classical composer or a
      contemporary rock composer

   A ten-part series on the life and work of your favorite sports figure

4. The local high-school video club has produced a music video, using magazine pictures that are synchronized with the latest recording of a rock band. The students plead with you to persuade the local cable company to put it on the air. What concerns, if any, do you have for airing this videotape? What can you do to accommodate the group's request?

# 18 The Director in Preproduction

## REVIEW OF KEY TERMS

*Match each term with its appropriate definition by filling in the corresponding bubble.*

1. **visualization**
2. **show format**
3. **fact sheet**

4. **treatment**
5. **fully scripted format**
6. **semiscripted format**

7. **storyboard**
8. **sequencing**
9. **locking-in**

**A.** A series of sketches of the key visualization points.

A ○ ○ ○ ○ ○
  1 2 3 4 5
  ○ ○ ○ ○
  6 7 8 9

**B.** Lists the items that have to be shown on-camera and their main features.

B ○ ○ ○ ○ ○
  1 2 3 4 5
  ○ ○ ○ ○
  6 7 8 9

**C.** The control and structuring of a series of shots.

C ○ ○ ○ ○ ○
  1 2 3 4 5
  ○ ○ ○ ○
  6 7 8 9

**D.** A script that contains complete dialogue and major visualization cues.

D ○ ○ ○ ○ ○
  1 2 3 4 5
  ○ ○ ○ ○
  6 7 8 9

**E.** The mental image of a shot or several key images of a sequence.

E ○ ○ ○ ○ ○
  1 2 3 4 5
  ○ ○ ○ ○
  6 7 8 9

PAGE TOTAL ☐

© 2006 Thomson Wadsworth

| 1. visualization | 4. treatment | 7. storyboard |
| 2. show format | 5. fully scripted format | 8. sequencing |
| 3. fact sheet | 6. semiscripted format | 9. locking-in |

**F.** A vivid visual or aural mental image during script analysis that determines subsequent visualizations and sequencing.

F  ○ ○ ○ ○ ○
   1  2  3  4  5
   ○ ○ ○ ○
   6  7  8  9

**G.** A brief narrative that tells what the program is about and what the audience is to see and hear.

G  ○ ○ ○ ○ ○
   1  2  3  4  5
   ○ ○ ○ ○
   6  7  8  9

**H.** A list of show segments in order of appearance.

H  ○ ○ ○ ○ ○
   1  2  3  4  5
   ○ ○ ○ ○
   6  7  8  9

**I.** A partial script that indicates major video cues in the left-hand column and partial dialogue and major audio cues in the right-hand column.

I  ○ ○ ○ ○ ○
   1  2  3  4  5
   ○ ○ ○ ○
   6  7  8  9

PAGE
TOTAL

SECTION
TOTAL

## REVIEW OF SCRIPT MARKING

1. Match each field-of-view designation with its appropriate full term by filling in the bubble with the corresponding number.

(10) cross-shot  
(11) over-the-shoulder shot  
(12) long shot  
(13) extreme close-up  
(14) medium shot  
(15) extreme long shot  
(16) close-up  
(17) medium close-up  
(18) two-shot  

a. CU

b. ECU

c. MCU

d. MS

e. O/S

f. X/S

g. 2-S

h. LS

i. ELS

**1a** ○ ○ ○ ○ ○
10 11 12 13 14
○ ○ ○ ○
15 16 17 18

**1b** ○ ○ ○ ○ ○
10 11 12 13 14
○ ○ ○ ○
15 16 17 18

**1c** ○ ○ ○ ○ ○
10 11 12 13 14
○ ○ ○ ○
15 16 17 18

**1d** ○ ○ ○ ○ ○
10 11 12 13 14
○ ○ ○ ○
15 16 17 18

**1e** ○ ○ ○ ○ ○
10 11 12 13 14
○ ○ ○ ○
15 16 17 18

**1f** ○ ○ ○ ○ ○
10 11 12 13 14
○ ○ ○ ○
15 16 17 18

**1g** ○ ○ ○ ○ ○
10 11 12 13 14
○ ○ ○ ○
15 16 17 18

**1h** ○ ○ ○ ○ ○
10 11 12 13 14
○ ○ ○ ○
15 16 17 18

**1i** ○ ○ ○ ○ ○
10 11 12 13 14
○ ○ ○ ○
15 16 17 18

PAGE TOTAL ☐

*Select the correct answers and fill in the bubbles with the corresponding numbers.*

**2.** The script markings in the following figure are (19) *acceptable*
(20) *unacceptable* because they (21) *are too small* (22) *have unnecessary or redundant cues* (23) *are in the wrong place* (24) *show large, essential cues.*
**(Fill in two bubbles.)**

JOHN

What's the matter?

*Ready camera 1*
*Ready to cue Tammy*

TAMMY

Nothing.

*Cue Tammy and*
*take camera 1*

JOHN

What do you mean, "nothing"? I can feel something is wrong.

TAMMY

*Ready to cue John*
*Ready to take camera 2*

Well, I am glad you have some feeling left.

JOHN   *Cue John and take*
*camera 2*

What's that supposed to mean?

TAMMY

Please, let's not start that again.

JOHN

Start what again?

TAMMY   *Ready to take camera 3*
*for a two-shot*

Well, I guess it's time to talk.   *Take camera 3*

JOHN

What do you think we have been doing all this time?

PAGE
TOTAL

SECTION
TOTAL

**3.** Mark the following show opening of a series on basic video production. Memorize the cues so that you can devote your attention primarily to the preview monitors rather than to the script.

---

```
VIDEO BASICS SERIES
SHOW NO. 7
TAPING DATE: July 15
AIR DATE: August 15


VIDEO                    AUDIO

VTR Opening              SOT (music)
:08 sec

CU of Phil               PHIL
                         Hi, I'm Phil Kipper. Welcome to the
                         Broadcast and Electronic Communication
                         Arts Series, "Video Basics." As
                         promised last week, we will take you to a
                         special room where magic takes place:
                         the editing suite.

Pull out to reveal       PHIL
editing suite. Phil      Let me introduce to you the magician in
introduces Hamid.        charge, Hamid Khani, whose official title
CU of Hamid.             is senior postproduction editor.


2-shot                   (SAYS HELLO TO HAMID AND HAS
                         HAMID SAY HELLO TO THE AUDIENCE)
```

---

4. Mark the following brief scene for a three-camera live-on-tape studio production or for a single-camera video-style production. Add any additional video cues you deem necessary. The scene takes place in the small office of a busy advertising executive. Draw a floor plan and prepare shot sheets.

```
                        KIM
                (Bursts into Gary's office)
        Let's go for coffee.

                        GARY
        I don't have time.

                        KIM
        Oh, shucks, make time.

                        GARY
        You seem to be in a good mood today.

                        KIM
        I'm always in a good mood...

                        GARY
        Especially when I'm around.

                        KIM
        I'm not so sure about that...but, yes, let's go.

                        GARY
        I really don't...

                        KIM
        (Walks behind Gary's desk and starts kissing his neck.)
        Don't what?

                        GARY
        Forget it. Let's go.

        (The telephone rings. Gary turns to answer it, but then lets it
        ring. He puts his arm around her. They both leave the office.)
```

## REVIEW OF INTERPRETATION
## OF PROCESS MESSAGES

1. A valuable process message should include  (25) *a specific audience*
   (26) *specific production equipment* (27) *the intended effect on the audience.*
   **(Multiple answers are possible.)**

   **1**  ○ ○ ○
        25  26  27

2. Evaluate to what extent the following four process messages will  (28) *greatly*
   (29) *moderately* (30) *inadequately*  help you visualize key show elements
   and provide  (31) *clear* (32) *moderately clear* (33) *not any or only very few*
   clues to the various medium requirements. **(Fill in two bubbles.)**

   **a.** The program should make people drive better.

   **2a**  ○ ○ ○
         28  29  30
         ○ ○ ○
         31  32  33

   **b.** The program should demonstrate to the target audience (daily commuters)
      the benefits of turn signals and the consequences of ignoring them in
      rush-hour traffic.

   **2b**  ○ ○ ○
         28  29  30
         ○ ○ ○
         31  32  33

   **c.** The program should help children learn some safety rules when walking
      to school.

   **2c**  ○ ○ ○
         28  29  30
         ○ ○ ○
         31  32  33

   **d.** This program is a series of comedy shows.

   **2d**  ○ ○ ○
         28  29  30
         ○ ○ ○
         31  32  33

   **e.** The program should make non–sports viewers admire, if not feel, the
      ballet-like skills of basketball players.

   **2e**  ○ ○ ○
         28  29  30
         ○ ○ ○
         31  32  33

   **f.** The program should show the skills of a racecar driver.

   **2f**  ○ ○ ○
         28  29  30
         ○ ○ ○
         31  32  33

PAGE TOTAL [     ]

**g.** The program should help people save water.

**h.** The program should show five different ways a family can save water during their morning shower and grooming.

## REVIEW OF INTERPRETING STORYBOARDS

1. Each of the following four storyboards shows one or several major problems. Fill in the bubbles whose numbers correspond with one or more of these major problems: (34) *poor continuity and disturbance of the mental map* (35) *wrong field-of-view designation* (36) *wrong above- or below-eye-level camera position.* **(Note: Storyboards may exhibit more than one problem.)**

### Storyboard a

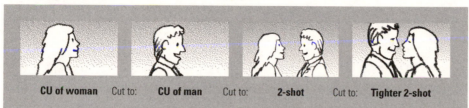

CU of woman   Cut to:   CU of man   Cut to:   2-shot   Cut to:   Tighter 2-shot

1a  ○ 34   ○ 35   ○ 36

### Storyboard b

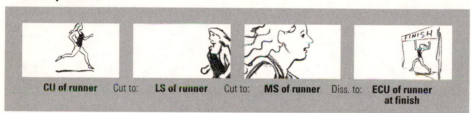

CU of runner   Cut to:   LS of runner   Cut to:   MS of runner   Diss. to:   ECU of runner at finish

1b  ○ 34   ○ 35   ○ 36

### Storyboard c

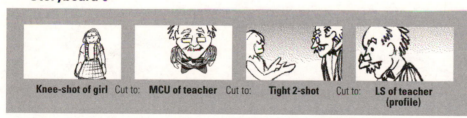

Knee-shot of girl  Cut to:  MCU of teacher  Cut to:  Tight 2-shot  Cut to:  LS of teacher (profile)

1c  ○ 34   ○ 35   ○ 36

### Storyboard d

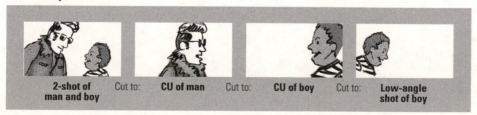

2-shot of man and boy   Cut to:   CU of man   Cut to:   CU of boy   Cut to:   Low-angle shot of boy

1d  ○ 34   ○ 35   ○ 36

SECTION TOTAL ☐

*Mark the following statements as true or false by filling in the bubbles in the*
***T** (for true) or **F** (for false) column.*

|   | | T | F |
|---|---|---|---|

1. Because the director is engaged in artistic activities, knowledge of the technical production aspects is relatively unimportant.  **1** ○ 37  ○ 38

2. Although the process message is important to the director in the production phase, it is relatively unimportant in preproduction.  **2** ○ 39  ○ 40

3. Proper visualization is essential for correct sequencing.  **3** ○ 41  ○ 42

4. A good floor plan will greatly facilitate camera and talent blocking.  **4** ○ 43  ○ 44

5. A fact sheet lists all camera shots in the left-hand column and all dialogue in the right-hand column.  **5** ○ 45  ○ 46

6. Good floor managers will cue on their own if they think the director missed a cue.  **6** ○ 47  ○ 48

7. When preparing camera shot sheets, the shots for each camera are listed in the order they appear in the script.  **7** ○ 49  ○ 50

8. If the script marking simply indicates "(2)" for one shot and "(3)" for the next, it implies that you should give a "Ready three" cue and then call for a "Take three."  **8** ○ 51  ○ 52

9. The locking-in point means that you conjure up a vivid visual or aural image while analyzing the script.  **9** ○ 53  ○ 54

10. A storyboard shows the key visualization points of an event.  **10** ○ 55  ○ 56

11. Dramas are always fully scripted.  **11** ○ 57  ○ 58

12. The drama script format requires the full dialogue of all actors but only a minimum of visualization cues.  **12** ○ 59  ○ 60

13. In a properly scripted documentary, all audio information is on page-left and all video information is on page-right.  **13** ○ 61  ○ 62

14. The fact, or rundown, sheet lists only points that the talent must mention in the ad-lib on-camera demonstration.  **14** ○ 63  ○ 64

15. In complex multicamera shows, the AD normally gives all standby cues.  **15** ○ 65  ○ 66

SECTION TOTAL ☐

## PROBLEM-SOLVING APPLICATIONS

1.  The executive producer tells you that she has cut the position of floor manager because the camera operator can do the cueing. What is your response?

2.  When asked to direct an on-location television adaptation of the current theater arts department stage play at the local park, you are advised that the director of the play will determine the number and the positions of the cameras because he, after all, knows the stage blocking better than you do. What is your reaction? What would you suggest?

3.  The director of a live-on-tape segment of a new situation comedy tells you, the producer, that she has great difficulty deciding on optimal camera positions and marking the script because the art director has not yet finished the floor plan. What is your reaction? What would you suggest?

4.  While you're directing an EFP of a documentary segment on the lumber industry, the producer tells you not to worry too much about shot continuity because he intends to put the show together in extensive postproduction editing. Do you agree with the producer? If so, why? If not, why not?

5.  The novice director proudly shows you, the producer, his marked show format for a live-on-tape studio interview. He wrote out in longhand all the ready and take cues, as well as all the VTR rolls and cues for special effects. His writing takes up more space than the information of the show format. What is your reaction? Why?

6.  The floor manager tells the new morning show director that the setup of scenery is the art director's job and not the floor manager's. What is your response?

7.  The director tells the floor manager to give some of the major cues in case he forgets to do so. What is your reaction? Why?

8.  The floor manager tells you, the director, not to worry about the time because she has done the show many times before and knows what time cues to give the talent. What will you tell the floor manager?

9.  During the rehearsal of a complex multicamera scene, the director tells you, the AD, to take over calling the shots while she watches the scene on the line monitor in the studio. Do you think this is a good idea? If so, why? If not, why not?

10. Observe the scene while riding on a bus or train, waiting in line at an airport, eating lunch in a cafeteria, or sitting in a classroom listening to a lecture. How would you re-create one or all of these scenes for a multicamera or single-camera production?

Course No. _____  Date _____  Name _____

# 19 The Director in Production and Postproduction

## REVIEW OF KEY TERMS

*Match each term with its appropriate definition by filling in the corresponding bubble.*

1. **subjective time**
2. **walk-through**
3. **camera rehearsal**
4. **dry run**
5. **multicamera directing**
6. **production schedule**
7. **clock, or schedule, time**
8. **intercom**
9. **single-camera directing**

**A.** The times when a program starts and stops.

A  ① ② ③ ④ ⑤
   ⑥ ⑦ ⑧ ⑨

**B.** An orientation session on the set with the production crew and talent.

B  ① ② ③ ④ ⑤
   ⑥ ⑦ ⑧ ⑨

**C.** A communication system widely used by all production and technical personnel so that they can communicate with one another during a show.

C  ① ② ③ ④ ⑤
   ⑥ ⑦ ⑧ ⑨

**D.** A full rehearsal with cameras and other pieces of production equipment.

D  ① ② ③ ④ ⑤
   ⑥ ⑦ ⑧ ⑨

**E.** The duration of time we feel.

E  ① ② ③ ④ ⑤
   ⑥ ⑦ ⑧ ⑨

PAGE TOTAL ☐

© 2006 Thomson Wadsworth

*Chapter 19 — The Director in Production and Postproduction*

1. subjective time
2. walk-through
3. camera rehearsal
4. dry run
5. multicamera directing
6. production schedule
7. clock, or schedule, time
8. intercom
9. single-camera directing

**F.** A schedule that shows the time periods allotted for various production activities.

F ⭕ ⭕ ⭕ ⭕ ⭕
  1   2   3   4   5
  ⭕ ⭕ ⭕ ⭕
  6   7   8   9

**G.** The simultaneous coordination of two or more cameras for instantaneous editing.

G ⭕ ⭕ ⭕ ⭕ ⭕
  1   2   3   4   5
  ⭕ ⭕ ⭕ ⭕
  6   7   8   9

**H.** A rehearsal without equipment.

H ⭕ ⭕ ⭕ ⭕ ⭕
  1   2   3   4   5
  ⭕ ⭕ ⭕ ⭕
  6   7   8   9

**I.** The coordination of a single camera for takes that are separately recorded for postproduction.

I ⭕ ⭕ ⭕ ⭕ ⭕
  1   2   3   4   5
  ⭕ ⭕ ⭕ ⭕
  6   7   8   9

PAGE TOTAL

SECTION TOTAL

## REVIEW OF DIRECTOR'S TERMINOLOGY

1. **Director's visualization cues.** From the list below, select the cue necessary to adjust the picture on the left screen to the picture on the right screen (in pairs from a through l) and fill in the bubbles with the corresponding numbers.

| | | |
|---|---|---|
| (10) tilt up | (15) zoom out | (19) pedestal up or |
| (11) tilt down | (16) truck right | crane up |
| (12) dolly in | (17) arc left | (20) pan left |
| (13) dolly out | (18) pedestal down | (21) pan right |
| (14) zoom in | or crane down | |

**a.**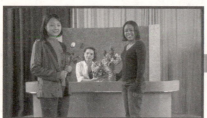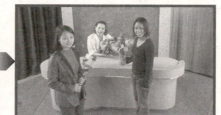

1a  ◯ ◯ ◯ ◯
    10 11 12 13
    ◯ ◯ ◯ ◯
    14 15 16 17
    ◯ ◯ ◯ ◯
    18 19 20 21

**b.**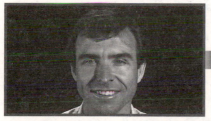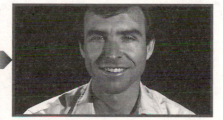

1b  ◯ ◯ ◯ ◯
    10 11 12 13
    ◯ ◯ ◯ ◯
    14 15 16 17
    ◯ ◯ ◯ ◯
    18 19 20 21

**c.**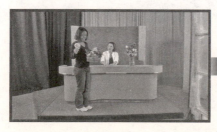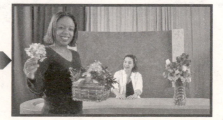

1c  ◯ ◯ ◯ ◯
    10 11 12 13
    ◯ ◯ ◯ ◯
    14 15 16 17
    ◯ ◯ ◯ ◯
    18 19 20 21

PAGE
TOTAL  [    ]

| (10) tilt up | (15) zoom out | (19) pedestal up or |
| (11) tilt down | (16) truck right | crane up |
| (12) dolly in | (17) arc left | (20) pan left |
| (13) dolly out | (18) pedestal down | (21) pan right |
| (14) zoom in | or crane down | |

d.

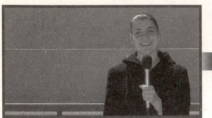

**1d**
○ ○ ○ ○
10 11 12 13
○ ○ ○ ○
14 15 16 17
○ ○ ○ ○
18 19 20 21

e.

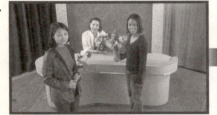

**1e**
○ ○ ○ ○
10 11 12 13
○ ○ ○ ○
14 15 16 17
○ ○ ○ ○
18 19 20 21

f.

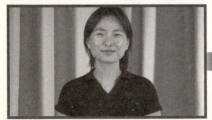

**1f**
○ ○ ○ ○
10 11 12 13
○ ○ ○ ○
14 15 16 17
○ ○ ○ ○
18 19 20 21

P A G E
T O T A L

g.
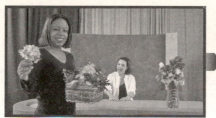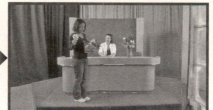

**1g**  ○ ○ ○ ○
10 11 12 13
○ ○ ○ ○
14 15 16 17
○ ○ ○ ○
18 19 20 21

h.
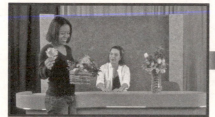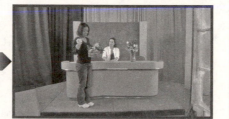

**1h**  ○ ○ ○ ○
10 11 12 13
○ ○ ○ ○
14 15 16 17
○ ○ ○ ○
18 19 20 21

i.
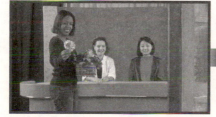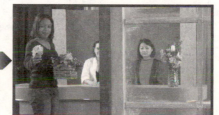

**1i**  ○ ○ ○ ○
10 11 12 13
○ ○ ○ ○
14 15 16 17
○ ○ ○ ○
18 19 20 21

j.
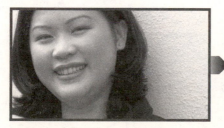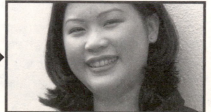

**1j**  ○ ○ ○ ○
10 11 12 13
○ ○ ○ ○
14 15 16 17
○ ○ ○ ○
18 19 20 21

PAGE
TOTAL  [    ]

*Chapter 19* — *The Director in Production and Postproduction*

| (10) tilt up | (15) zoom out | (19) pedestal up or |
| (11) tilt down | (16) truck right | crane up |
| (12) dolly in | (17) arc left | (20) pan left |
| (13) dolly out | (18) pedestal down | (21) pan right |
| (14) zoom in | or crane down | |

**k.**

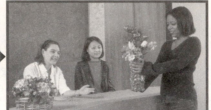

1k  ○ ○ ○ ○
    10  11  12  13
    ○ ○ ○ ○
    14  15  16  17
    ○ ○ ○ ○
    18  19  20  21

**l.**

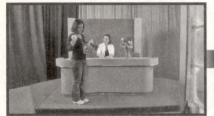

1l  ○ ○ ○ ○
    10  11  12  13
    ○ ○ ○ ○
    14  15  16  17
    ○ ○ ○ ○
    18  19  20  21

**2. Director's cues to floor manager concerning the positioning of props.**

Select the appropriate cue to the floor manager to adjust the position of the prop shown on the left screen to that of the right screen and fill in the bubbles with the corresponding numbers.

(22) turn it clockwise
(23) turn it counterclockwise

**a.**

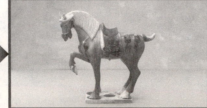

2a  ○      ○
    22      23

PAGE
TOTAL [      ]

*Chapter 19* — *The Director in Production and Postproduction*

**Director's cues to floor manager concerning the positioning of talent.**
From the list below, select the appropriate cue to the floor manager to adjust the position of the talent shown on the left screen to that of the right screen (in pairs b through d) and fill in the bubbles with the corresponding numbers.

(24) move talent to camera right
(25) pan right

**b.**

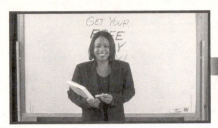 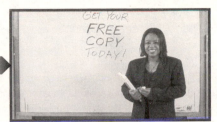

2b  ○   ○
    24   25

(26) have talent turn in (toward the camera)
(27) have talent move left

**c.**

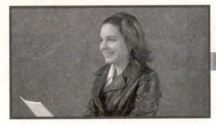 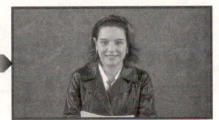

2c  ○   ○
    26   27

(28) have woman turn to her left
(29) have camera arc right

**d.**

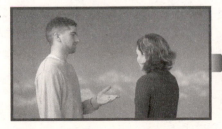 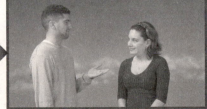

2d  ○   ○
    28   29

PAGE
TOTAL [        ]

**3.** From the list below, select the correct director's cues for transitions by filling in the corresponding bubbles. *(Multiple answers are possible.)*

(30) Ready to take camera two. Take camera two.
(31) Ready three. Take three.
(32) Ready one. Dissolve to one.
(33) Ready to go to black. Go to black.
(34) Ready wipe. Dissolve to two.
(35) Ready to change C.G. page. Change page.

**3**  ○ 30  ○ 31  ○ 32  ○ 33  ○ 34  ○ 35

**4.** From the list below, select the director who uses the correct sequence of cues for the opening of a two-camera (C1 and C2) interview and fill in the corresponding bubble. *(There is a title key for the guest. Assume that the crew has received a general standby cue and that bars and tone have already been recorded on the tape by the AD.)*

(36) *Director A:* "Ready to take C.G. Slate. Take slate. Ready black. Black. Beeper. Ready to come up on one CU of host—take one. Cue host. Ready two [on guest]. Take two. Cue guest. Key title. Take one."

(37) *Director B:* "Ready to roll VTR. Roll VTR. Ready C.G. Slate. Take C.G. Read slate. Ready black. Change page [C.G.]. Ready beeper. To black. Beeper. One, CU of host. Ready to come up on one. Open mic, cue host, up on one. Two, CU of guest. Ready two. Ready to key C.G. Take two, key. Lose key. Ready one, two-shot. Take one."

(38) *Director C:* "Ready to roll VTR. Roll VTR. Ready C.G. Slate. Read slate. Ready black. Ready beeper. To black. Beeper. Ready to come up on one. Up on one. Ready two. Take two. Key. Lose key. Ready one. Take one."

**4**  ○ 36  ○ 37  ○ 38

**5.** From the list below, select the correct director's cues to the floor manager by filling in the corresponding bubbles. *(Multiple answers are possible.)*

(39) Ready to cue Mary. Cue Mary.
(40) Ready to cue him. Cue him.
(41) Make him talk faster.
(42) Move her stage-right.
(43) Turn the can counterclockwise.
(44) Have two of them come to a close.

**5**  ○ 39  ○ 40  ○ 41  ○ 42  ○ 43  ○ 44

PAGE TOTAL ⬚

SECTION TOTAL ⬚

## REVIEW OF REHEARSAL TECHNIQUES

*Select the correct answers and fill in the bubbles with the corresponding numbers.*

1.  Camera rehearsal is conducted  (45) *similar to a dress rehearsal*  (46) *for cameras only*  (47) *for all technical operations, but without talent.*

    **1**  ○ 45  ○ 46  ○ 47

2.  If pressed for time, you should call for  (48) *an uninterrupted camera rehearsal* (49) *a blocking rehearsal*  (50) *a walk-through/camera rehearsal combination.*

    **2**  ○ 48  ○ 49  ○ 50

3.  Blocking rehearsals are most efficiently conducted from  (51) *the control room* (52) *the studio floor or rehearsal hall*  (53) *on the actual studio set.*

    **3**  ○ 51  ○ 52  ○ 53

4.  Rehearsals that combine walk-throughs and camera rehearsal are most efficiently conducted from the  (54) *studio floor*  (55) *rehearsal hall* (56) *control room.*

    **4**  ○ 54  ○ 55  ○ 56

5.  When engaged in EFP, you need not worry about  (57) *talent and technical walk-throughs*  (58) *cross-overs from one location to the next*  (59) *the various camera positions.*

    **5**  ○ 57  ○ 58  ○ 59

6.  When doing a walk-through/camera rehearsal combination from the studio floor, you should give  (60) *all cues as though you were directing from the control room*  (61) *only the talent cues*  (62) *only the camera cues.*

    **6**  ○ 60  ○ 61  ○ 62

7.  When scheduling "notes" segments in your time line, you need to also schedule  (63) *additional talent rehearsal time*  (64) *reset time*  (65) *additional technical rehearsal time.*

    **7**  ○ 63  ○ 64  ○ 65

8.  When calling for a "take," you should pause between the "read" and the "take" cues  (66) *as little as possible*  (67) *until you see the TD put his finger on the right switcher button*  (68) *for at least five seconds.*

    **8**  ○ 66  ○ 67  ○ 68

9.  When doing a single-camera ENG or EFP, you should  (69) *always get a fair amount of cutaways*  (70) *get cutaways only if you think your shots will not cut together well*  (71) *not bother with cutaways if you have plenty of time for postproduction.*

    **9**  ○ 69  ○ 70  ○ 71

10. When breaking down an EFP script for a single-camera production, you should (72) *try to maintain the narrative order of the scenes*  (73) *combine all scenes that play at the same location and/or with the same talent*  (74) *start with the most interesting parts to take advantage of the talent's creative energy.*

    **10**  ○ 72  ○ 73  ○ 74

**SECTION TOTAL** [ ]

**1.** Assume that the following six shots represent a sequence of video inputs on the preview monitor in the order you will switch them to the line-out. Using the floor plan below, specify the cameras and the other video inputs used for the shots. Note that one video input does not originate in the studio and another uses two video sources simultaneously.

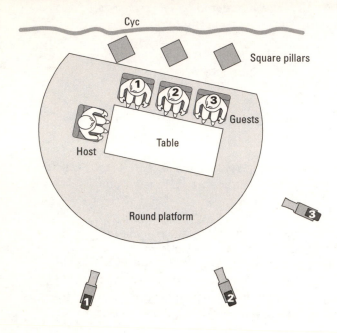

Sources:    (75) Camera 1

(76) Camera 2

(77) Camera 3

(78) Videotape 1

(79) C.G.

**a.**

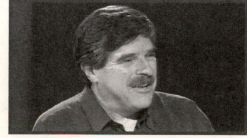

Host

1a  ◯ ◯ ◯ ◯ ◯
    75  76  77  78  79

PAGE TOTAL ☐

**b.**

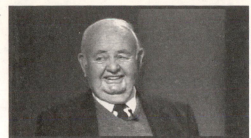

Guest 1

**c.**

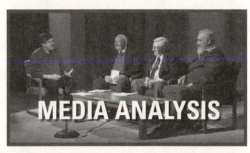

MEDIA ANALYSIS

**d.**

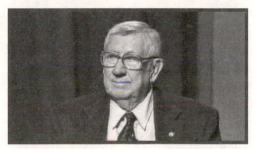

Guest 2

**e.**

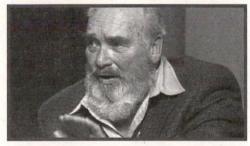

Guest 3

**f.**

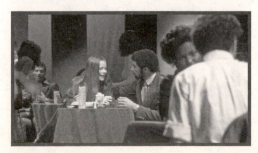

**2.** Each of these time-line listings is (80) *acceptable* (81) *unacceptable,* because (82) *the time allotted for this production activity is appropriate* (83) *it allots too much time for the specific production activity* (84) *it allots too little time for the specific production activity.* **(Fill in two bubbles.)**

**a. Time Line May 25:** Live-on-tape 20-minute interview with college president on a standard interview set. She brings a model of the new library building, which needs to be set up in an adjacent area.

| | | | |
|---|---|---|---|
| (1) | 8:15 a.m. | Crew call | 2a (1) ○ ○<br>80 81<br>○ ○ ○<br>82 83 84 |
| (2) | 8:30–9:00 a.m. | Tech meeting | 2a (2) ○ ○<br>80 81<br>○ ○ ○<br>82 83 84 |
| (3) | 9:00–11:00 a.m. | Setup and lighting | 2a (3) ○ ○<br>80 81<br>○ ○ ○<br>82 83 84 |
| (4) | 11:00–11:30 a.m. | Lunch | 2a (4) ○ ○<br>80 81<br>○ ○ ○<br>82 83 84 |
| (5) | 11:30–11:45 a.m. | Notes and reset | 2a (5) ○ ○<br>80 81<br>○ ○ ○<br>82 83 84 |
| (6) | 11:45 a.m.–12:00 p.m. | Briefing of president (Green Room) | 2a (6) ○ ○<br>80 81<br>○ ○ ○<br>82 83 84 |
| (7) | 12:00–12:30 p.m. | Run-through and camera rehearsal | 2a (7) ○ ○<br>80 81<br>○ ○ ○<br>82 83 84 |
| (8) | 12:30–12:45 p.m. | Notes | 2a (8) ○ ○<br>80 81<br>○ ○ ○<br>82 83 84 |
| (9) | 12:45–1:00 p.m. | Reset | 2a (9) ○ ○<br>80 81<br>○ ○ ○<br>82 83 84 |

P A G E
T O T A L

*Chapter 19* — *The Director in Production and Postproduction*

(10)  1:00–1:10 p.m.          Break

**2a (10)**  ○ ○
80 81
○ ○ ○
82 83 84

(11)  1:10–1:45 p.m.          Tape

**2a (11)**  ○ ○
80 81
○ ○ ○
82 83 84

(12)  1:45–1:55 p.m.          Spill

**2a (12)**  ○ ○
80 81
○ ○ ○
82 83 84

(13)  1:55–2:10 p.m.          Strike

**2a (13)**  ○ ○
80 81
○ ○ ○
82 83 84

**b. Time Line June 2:** Multicamera shoot for postproduction of two songs by a local rock group.

(1)  6:00 a.m.                Crew call

**2b (1)**  ○ ○
80 81
○ ○ ○
82 83 84

(2)  6:15–6:35 a.m.           Tech meeting

**2b (2)**  ○ ○
80 81
○ ○ ○
82 83 84

(3)  6:35–7:00 a.m.           Setup and lighting

**2b (3)**  ○ ○
80 81
○ ○ ○
82 83 84

(4)  7:00–9:30 a.m.           Production meeting

**2b (4)**  ○ ○
80 81
○ ○ ○
82 83 84

(5)  9:30 a.m.–12:30 p.m.     First run-through with cameras

**2b (5)**  ○ ○
80 81
○ ○ ○
82 83 84

PAGE TOTAL [     ]

© 2006 Thomson Wadsworth

(6)  12:30–2:30 p.m.        Lunch                           **2b** (6)  ○  ○
                                                                      80  81
                                                                   ○  ○  ○
                                                                   82  83  84

(7)  2:30–2:45 p.m.         Tape first song                 **2b** (7)  ○  ○
                                                                      80  81
                                                                   ○  ○  ○
                                                                   82  83  84

(8)  2:45–3:30 p.m.         Notes and reset                 **2b** (8)  ○  ○
                                                                      80  81
                                                                   ○  ○  ○
                                                                   82  83  84

(9)  3:30–5:00 p.m.         Tape second song                **2b** (9)  ○  ○
                                                                      80  81
                                                                   ○  ○  ○
                                                                   82  83  84

(10) 5:00–6:00 p.m.         Strike                          **2b** (10)  ○  ○
                                                                      80  81
                                                                   ○  ○  ○
                                                                   82  83  84

P A G E
T O T A L   _____

SECTION
TOTAL   _____

*Chapter 19* — *The Director in Production and Postproduction*

# REVIEW OF TIMING

*Select the correct answers and fill in the bubbles with the corresponding numbers.*

1. In the noon newscast, you must switch to the first 3-minute satellite feed at exactly 3:45 minutes into the show and the second feed at 15:15 minutes after the end of the first one. You need to switch to the remote feeds at:

   (85) 12:03:45 and 12:19:00
   (86) 12:03:45 and 12:22:00
   (87) 12:03:45 and 12:15:15

   **1** ○ ○ ○
      85   86   87

2. The log indicates that the *Women: Face-to-face* program ends at 11:26:30. A large part of the program is taken up by a fashion show. The fashion coordinator would like a 1-minute, a 30-second, and a 15-second cue, as well as a cut at the end of her segment. The regular program host, who follows the fashion show with a 1½-minute closing, would like a 30-second and a 15-second cue and a cut at the end of the program. From the list below, select the correct clock times for the cues.

   (88) 11:24:00, 11:24:30, 11:24:45, 11:25:00 and 11:26:00, 11:26:15, 11:26:30
   (89) 11:24:30, 11:25:00, 11:25:45, 11:26:00 and 11:26:15, 11:26:30
   (90) 11:22:00, 11:23:00, 11:24:00, 11:24:30 and 11:25:00, 11:26:00, 11:26:15

   **2** ○ ○ ○
      88   89   90

3. In subjective timing pace refers to (91) *the beat of the show segment* (92) *how fast or slow it seems to move* (93) *how the parts of the segment relate to one another.*

   **3** ○ ○ ○
      91   92   93

4. In subjective timing rhythm refers to (94) *the beat we feel when watching the segment* (95) *how fast or slow the segment feels* (96) *the relative intensity of the segment.*

   **4** ○ ○ ○
      94   95   96

SECTION TOTAL [ ]

# REVIEW QUIZ

Mark the following statements as true or false by filling in the bubbles in the
**T** (for true) or **F** (for false) column.

|  |  | T | F |
|---|---|---|---|
| **1.** | Keeping accurate running time is more important in directing a live multicamera show than a single-camera EFP. | 1 ○ 97 | ○ 98 |
| **2.** | When directing a studio show, the S.A. system is more appropriate than the P.L. system. | 2 ○ 99 | ○ 100 |
| **3.** | During a walk-through/camera rehearsal combination, the director rehearses primarily from the studio floor. | 3 ○ 101 | ○ 102 |
| **4.** | When directing from the control room, you should address the name of the camera operator rather than the camera number to get efficient camera action. | 4 ○ 103 | ○ 104 |
| **5.** | When directing a fully scripted show, you should pay more attention to the script than the preview or line monitors. | 5 ○ 105 | ○ 106 |
| **6.** | When doing an EFP, the talent and technical walk-throughs are less important than when doing a studio show. | 6 ○ 107 | ○ 108 |
| **7.** | When directing a daily newscast, you do not need a floor plan to preplan the camera shots. | 7 ○ 109 | ○ 110 |
| **8.** | You should tell the floor manager whenever there is a technical problem that you need to solve from the control room. | 8 ○ 111 | ○ 112 |
| **9.** | Even when doing an EFP, you should check the videotape to see whether the preceding scene was properly recorded before moving to the next location. | 9 ○ 113 | ○ 114 |
| **10.** | Cutaways are especially important in film-style shooting. | 10 ○ 115 | ○ 116 |
| **11.** | When directing a single-camera EFP, a properly working intercom system is one of the most essential setup items. | 11 ○ 117 | ○ 118 |
| **12.** | Even with an efficient intercom system, the switcher should be located right next to the director's position. | 12 ○ 119 | ○ 120 |
| **13.** | To save time in a studio rehearsal, you should use the S.A. system as often as possible. | 13 ○ 121 | ○ 122 |
| **14.** | There should be no other activities scheduled between the "notes" and "reset" segments of the time line. | 14 ○ 123 | ○ 124 |
| **15.** | If possible, you should rehearse the show segments in the order in which they are to be taped. | 15 ○ 125 | ○ 126 |

**SECTION TOTAL** [ ]

## PROBLEM-SOLVING APPLICATIONS

1. Mark a scene from a fully scripted TV play and practice calling the shots.

2. During the videotaping of the first scene of a demanding outdoor EFP for a car commercial, the audio person suggests doing a retake because she picked up a brief, distant jet sound. Would you recommend a retake? If so, why? If not, why not?

3. During the evening news, the wrong VTR story comes up. What can you do?

4. During an O/S sequence in a multicamera dramatic production, one of the actors has trouble hitting the blocking marks and is frequently obscured by the camera-near person. What advice would you give the actor?

5. The experienced news editor tells you, the director, not to worry about the scene that is to apply complexity editing to show the mounting psychological confusion of one of the characters in a docudrama. After all, she has been editing news for four years now and should know how shots go together. What is your concern? Why?

6. The director uses one set of commands during rehearsal but switches to another when doing the on-the-air show. Which potential problems do you foresee, if any? Be specific.

7. The producer suggests that you not waste valuable time by doing a walk-through/camera rehearsal from the studio floor but skip right to the camera rehearsal from the control room. What is your reaction? Why?

8. When checking all the intercom systems before a remote live telecast of a large political gathering at city hall, the talent's I.F.B. interrupts itself from time to time. What backup cueing device would you recommend that close to airtime?

9. When pressed for time, the director tells you, the line producer, that he will conduct the rehearsal from the studio floor. Would you agree or disagree with such a move? Be specific. How, if at all, would the director's request affect the studio equipment and control room activities?

10. The floor manager expresses her concern to you, the director, about the lack of adequate intercom facilities for an EFP of the local garden show. How would you respond?

# 20 Field Production and Big Remotes

## REVIEW OF KEY TERMS

*Match each term with its appropriate definition by filling in the corresponding bubble.*

1. broadband
2. Ku-band
3. mini-link
4. big remote

5. remote survey
6. uplink
7. downlink
8. instant replay

9. microwave relay
10. location sketch
11. DBS
12. iso camera

**A.** Repeating a key play or an important event for the viewer, through playing back by videotape or disk-stored video, immediately after its live occurrence.

A
○ ○ ○ ○
1 2 3 4
○ ○ ○ ○
5 6 7 8
○ ○ ○ ○
9 10 11 12

**B.** A high-frequency signal used by satellites.

B
○ ○ ○ ○
1 2 3 4
○ ○ ○ ○
5 6 7 8
○ ○ ○ ○
9 10 11 12

**C.** A variety of information sent simultaneously over a fiber-optic cable.

C
○ ○ ○ ○
1 2 3 4
○ ○ ○ ○
5 6 7 8
○ ○ ○ ○
9 10 11 12

**D.** A signal transport from the remote location to the station or transmitter in various transmission steps.

D
○ ○ ○ ○
1 2 3 4
○ ○ ○ ○
5 6 7 8
○ ○ ○ ○
9 10 11 12

PAGE TOTAL [ ]

| 1. broadband | 5. remote survey | 9. microwave relay |
|---|---|---|
| 2. Ku-band | 6. uplink | 10. location sketch |
| 3. mini-link | 7. downlink | 11. DBS |
| 4. big remote | 8. instant replay | 12. iso camera |

**E.** A production outside the studio to televise live and/or record live-on-tape a large scheduled event.

E
○ ○ ○ ○
1 2 3 4
○ ○ ○ ○
5 6 7 8
○ ○ ○ ○
9 10 11 12

**F.** A preproduction on-location investigation of the existing facilities of a scheduled telecast away from the studio.

F
○ ○ ○ ○
1 2 3 4
○ ○ ○ ○
5 6 7 8
○ ○ ○ ○
9 10 11 12

**G.** A rough map of the locale of a remote telecast.

G
○ ○ ○ ○
1 2 3 4
○ ○ ○ ○
5 6 7 8
○ ○ ○ ○
9 10 11 12

**H.** A satellite with a high-powered transponder.

H
○ ○ ○ ○
1 2 3 4
○ ○ ○ ○
5 6 7 8
○ ○ ○ ○
9 10 11 12

**I.** An earth station transmitter used to send video and audio signals to a satellite.

I
○ ○ ○ ○
1 2 3 4
○ ○ ○ ○
5 6 7 8
○ ○ ○ ○
9 10 11 12

PAGE TOTAL

| 1. broadband | 5. remote survey | 9. microwave relay |
|---|---|---|
| 2. Ku-band | 6. uplink | 10. location sketch |
| 3. mini-link | 7. downlink | 11. DBS |
| 4. big remote | 8. instant replay | 12. iso camera |

**J.** An antenna and equipment that receives the signals coming from a satellite.

J
○ ○ ○ ○
1  2  3  4
○ ○ ○ ○
5  6  7  8
○ ○ ○ ○
9 10 11 12

**K.** A setup of several small microwave transmitters and receivers to transport the television signal around obstacles.

K
○ ○ ○ ○
1  2  3  4
○ ○ ○ ○
5  6  7  8
○ ○ ○ ○
9 10 11 12

**L.** Often used in sports remotes. Feeds into the switcher and its own VTR.

L
○ ○ ○ ○
1  2  3  4
○ ○ ○ ○
5  6  7  8
○ ○ ○ ○
9 10 11 12

PAGE TOTAL [    ]

SECTION TOTAL [    ]

## REVIEW OF REMOTE PRODUCTION FEATURES

*Select the correct answers and fill in the bubbles with the corresponding numbers.*

1. The most flexible type of field production that needs little or no preproduction is (13) *ENG* (14) *EFP* (15) *big remotes.*

   **1** ○ ○ ○
      13   14   15

2. Using multiple cameras or camcorders in EFP means that they (16) *run in sync* (17) *must feed a switcher* (18) *shoot a scene simultaneously.*

   **2** ○ ○ ○
      16   17   18

3. A complex intercommunication system is most important for (19) *ENG* (20) *EFP* (21) *big remotes.*

   **3** ○ ○ ○
      19   20   21

4. The remote system least likely to use signal transmission equipment is (22) *ENG* (23) *EFP* (24) *big remotes.*

   **4** ○ ○ ○
      22   23   24

5. The normal transmission equipment in ENG vans is (25) *a microwave transmitter* (26) *a satellite uplink* (27) *fiber-optic cable.*

   **5** ○ ○ ○
      25   26   27

6. The directing procedure that most closely resembles multicamera studio production is (28) *ENG* (29) *EFP* (30) *big remotes.*

   **6** ○ ○ ○
      28   29   30

7. The walk-through rehearsal is least important for (31) *ENG* (32) *EFP* (33) *big remotes.*

   **7** ○ ○ ○
      31   32   33

8. A big-remote survey requires (34) *only a production survey* (35) *only a technical survey* (36) *both a production and a technical survey.*

   **8** ○ ○ ○
      34   35   36

9. To ensure access to the event location, you need (37) *a contact person* (38) *a written statement from the producer* (39) *an OK from the chief of police.*

   **9** ○ ○ ○
      37   38   39

10. Because the camera setup is done by technical personnel, the director is (40) *not needed* (41) *very important* (42) *consulted only in emergencies* for the specific locations of the key cameras.

    **10** ○ ○ ○
       40   41   42

SECTION TOTAL [ ]

## REVIEW OF BIG REMOTES

1. Analyze the following five location sketches for field productions and big remotes. Evaluate the type and the position of each camera by the criteria listed below and fill in the bubbles with the corresponding numbers. *(Multiple answers are possible.)*

(43) camera position OK
(44) wrong or unnecessary camera position
(45) inappropriate camera type
(46) cable hazard
(47) lighting problems (shooting into the sun or against another strong light source)

Key for camera type:

ENG/EFP camera or camcorder    Studio/field camera

© 2006 Thomson Wadsworth

(43) camera position OK
(44) wrong or unnecessary camera position
(45) inappropriate camera type
(46) cable hazard
(47) lighting problems (shooting into the sun or against another
     strong light source)

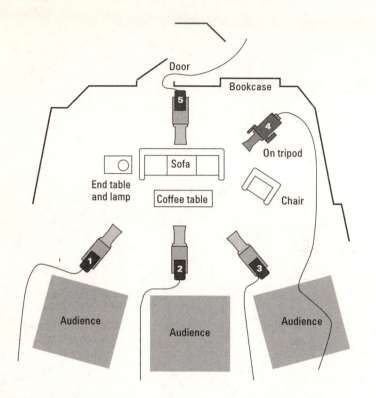

## Play

Videotaping of two performances of a high-school play (situation comedy) with a live audience, minimal postproduction, and the use of a large remote truck

**a.** Comments on C1

**b.** Comments on C2

**c.** Comments on C3

**d.** Comments on C4

**e.** Comments on C5

1a  C1  ○ ○ ○
        43 44 45
        ○ ○
        46 47

1b  C2  ○ ○ ○
        43 44 45
        ○ ○
        46 47

1c  C3  ○ ○ ○
        43 44 45
        ○ ○
        46 47

1d  C4  ○ ○ ○
        43 44 45
        ○ ○
        46 47

1e  C5  ○ ○ ○
        43 44 45
        ○ ○
        46 47

PAGE
TOTAL [   ]

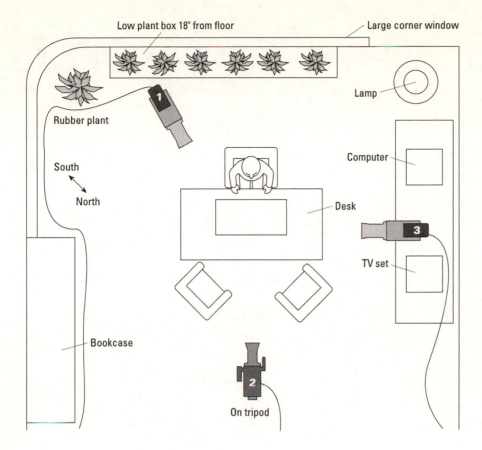

Low plant box 18" from floor

Large corner window

Lamp

Rubber plant

South

North

1

Desk

Computer

3

TV set

Bookcase

2

On tripod

**EFP of Company President's Address to Employees**
Live-on-tape or minimal postproduction
VTR date: July 15
VTR time: 2:30 p.m. to 4:30 p.m.
Place: President's office, Tower Building, 34th floor

    **f.** Comments on C1

    **g.** Comments on C2

    **h.** Comments on C3

**1f** **C1** ○ ○ ○
      43 44 45
      ○ ○
      46 47

**1g** **C2** ○ ○ ○
      43 44 45
      ○ ○
      46 47

**1h** **C3** ○ ○ ○
      43 44 45
      ○ ○
      46 47

PAGE
TOTAL

(43) camera position OK
(44) wrong or unnecessary camera position
(45) inappropriate camera type
(46) cable hazard
(47) lighting problems (shooting into the sun or against another strong light source)

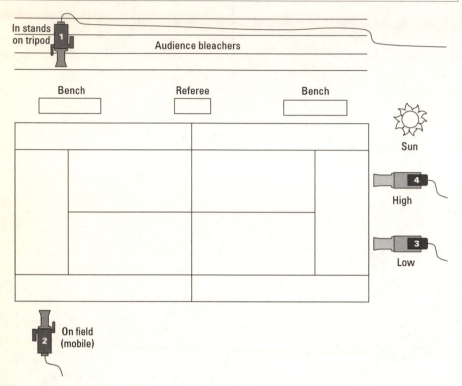

## Tennis Match
Live coverage of tennis match

**i.** Comments on C1

**j.** Comments on C2

**k.** Comments on C3

**l.** Comments on C4

| | | | | |
|---|---|---|---|---|
| **1i** | **C1** | ○ 43 | ○ 44 | ○ 45 |
| | | ○ 46 | ○ 47 | |
| **1j** | **C2** | ○ 43 | ○ 44 | ○ 45 |
| | | ○ 46 | ○ 47 | |
| **1k** | **C3** | ○ 43 | ○ 44 | ○ 45 |
| | | ○ 46 | ○ 47 | |
| **1l** | **C4** | ○ 43 | ○ 44 | ○ 45 |
| | | ○ 46 | ○ 47 | |

PAGE TOTAL

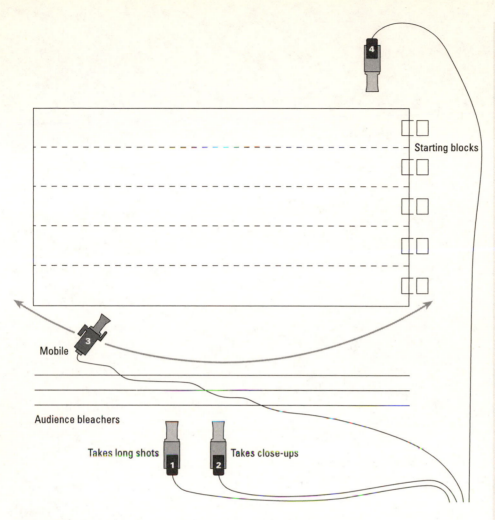

Starting blocks

Mobile

Audience bleachers

Takes long shots        Takes close-ups

**Swim Meet**
Live telecast of state swim meet; large indoor pool

    **m.** Comments on C1

    **n.** Comments on C2

    **o.** Comments on C3

    **p.** Comments on C4

**1m C1** ○ ○ ○
      43 44 45
      ○ ○
      46 47

**1n C2** ○ ○ ○
      43 44 45
      ○ ○
      46 47

**1o C3** ○ ○ ○
      43 44 45
      ○ ○
      46 47

**1p C4** ○ ○ ○
      43 44 45
      ○ ○
      46 47

PAGE
TOTAL

(43) camera position OK
(44) wrong or unnecessary camera position
(45) inappropriate camera type
(46) cable hazard
(47) lighting problems (shooting into the sun or against another strong light source)

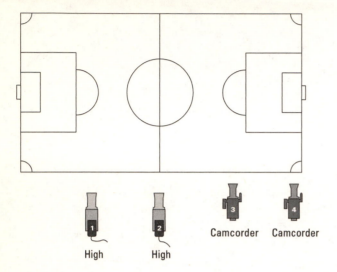

## Soccer Practice
EFP of soccer practice for a show that demonstrates the beauty and grace of a soccer game; heavy postproduction with effects and sound track

**q.** Comments on C1

1q  C1  ◯ ◯ ◯
          43  44  45
        ◯ ◯
          46  47

**r.** Comments on C2

1r  C2  ◯ ◯ ◯
          43  44  45
        ◯ ◯
          46  47

**s.** Comments on C3

1s  C3  ◯ ◯ ◯
          43  44  45
        ◯ ◯
          46  47

**t.** Comments on C4

1t  C4  ◯ ◯ ◯
          43  44  45
        ◯ ◯
          46  47

PAGE TOTAL [        ]

SECTION TOTAL [        ]

## ■ REVIEW OF FACILITIES REQUESTS

*Evaluate the equipment facilities requests for the three EFPs described below. Identify the **wrong** equipment and the items **not** needed and fill in the bubbles with the corresponding numbers. **Multiple answers are possible.***

**1.** Taped interview of a media scholar in his hotel room for news item

**1**  ○ ○ ○ ○ ○
48 49 50 51 52
○ ○ ○ ○
53 54 55 56

**Facilities Request 1**
(48) camcorder
(49) iso VTR
(50) portable lighting kit
(51) RCU
(52) 2 lavaliere mics
(53) portable audio mixer
(54) videotape
(55) batteries
(56) preview monitors

**2.** Midmorning taping of a brief dance number in front of city hall for a music video using ENG/EFP cameras, *not* camcorders

**2**  ○ ○ ○ ○ ○
57 58 59 60 61
○ ○ ○ ○
62 63 64 65

**Facilities Request 2**
(57) 3 ENG/EFP cameras
(58) 6 shotgun mics
(59) ESS
(60) 3 VTRs
(61) 3 RCUs, connecting cables, and portable monitors
(62) large audio mixer
(63) P.A. audiotape playback system
(64) portable lighting kit
(65) C.G.

**3.** Live stand-up traffic report from downtown during the afternoon rush hour

**3**  ○ ○ ○ ○ ○
66 67 68 69 70
○ ○ ○ ○
71 72 73 74

**Facilities Request 3**
(66) ENG camera
(67) 2 VTRs
(68) shotgun mic (camera mic)
(69) hand mic
(70) 3 portable lighting kits
(71) audiotape recorder
(72) microwave transmission equipment
(73) I.F.B. intercom
(74) C.G.

© 2006 Thomson Wadsworth

**SECTION TOTAL** [  ]

# REVIEW OF SIGNAL DISTRIBUTION SYSTEMS AND COMMUNICATION SATELLITES

*Select the correct answers and fill in the bubbles with the corresponding numbers.*

1. Small uplink trucks use (75) *the Ku-band* (76) *the C-band* (77) *their own satellite frequency* for signal transmission.

2. EFP makes (78) *more-frequent use of satellite transmission than* (79) *less-frequent use of satellite transmission than* (80) *about the same amount of satellite transmission as* big remotes.

3. A microwave signal (81) *can* (82) *cannot* be blocked by big buildings or mountains.

4. A mini-link refers to (83) *a small uplink* (84) *a small downlink* (85) *several microwave links to transport the signal around an obstacle.*

5. The C-band uplink and downlink dishes are (86) *the same as* (87) *smaller than* (88) *larger than* the ones for the Ku-band.

6. The Ku-band operates on (89) *a higher* (90) *a lower* (91) *the same* frequency as the C-band and is (92) *more stable in bad weather* (93) *less stable in bad weather* (94) *immune to weather conditions.* **(Fill in two bubbles.)**

| | | | |
|---|---|---|---|
| **1** | ○ 75 | ○ 76 | ○ 77 |
| **2** | ○ 78 | ○ 79 | ○ 80 |
| **3** | ○ 81 | ○ 82 | |
| **4** | ○ 83 | ○ 84 | ○ 85 |
| **5** | ○ 86 | ○ 87 | ○ 88 |
| **6** | ○ 89 | ○ 90 | ○ 91 |
| | ○ 92 | ○ 93 | ○ 94 |

SECTION TOTAL [       ]

## REVIEW QUIZ

*Mark the following statements as true or false by filling in the bubbles in the* **T** *(for true) or* **F** *(for false) column.*

|  |  | T | F |
|---|---|---|---|
| 1. | You need a switcher when using three EFP cameras as multiple isos. | **1** ○ 95 | ○ 96 |
| 2. | Remote surveys are relatively unimportant for EFP. | **2** ○ 97 | ○ 98 |
| 3. | If possible, you should do the survey for an outdoor remote during the time the actual production will take place. | **3** ○ 99 | ○ 100 |
| 4. | When shooting single-camera EFP for postproduction, you do not need extensive intercom systems. | **4** ○ 101 | ○ 102 |
| 5. | Remote surveys are relatively unimportant for ENG. | **5** ○ 103 | ○ 104 |
| 6. | So long as you have a good transmission system, you do not need VTRs in the remote truck. | **6** ○ 105 | ○ 106 |
| 7. | Cameras used for the regular coverage of a remote telecast cannot be used for instant replay. | **7** ○ 107 | ○ 108 |
| 8. | So long as you use an I.F.B. system, the floor manager is unnecessary for big remotes. | **8** ○ 109 | ○ 110 |
| 9. | The contact person is important only in preproduction. | **9** ○ 111 | ○ 112 |
| 10. | So long as you have good headsets, you do not need other intercom systems on big remotes. | **10** ○ 113 | ○ 114 |
| 11. | To make the remote telecast as exciting as possible, you should use as many cameras as are available. | **11** ○ 115 | ○ 116 |
| 12. | Big-remote trucks usually contain an audio control center, a video control center, a production control center, a videotape room, a video control center, and transmission area. | **12** ○ 117 | ○ 118 |
| 13. | The C.G. operation is especially important during a live pickup of a football game. | **13** ○ 119 | ○ 120 |
| 14. | A careful audio setup is as important as the camera setup in big remotes. | **14** ○ 121 | ○ 122 |

SECTION TOTAL [    ]

## PROBLEM-SOLVING APPLICATIONS

1. Conduct a detailed remote survey for the live coverage of one of the following: (1) a football game, (2) a track meet, (3) a basketball game, (4) a baseball game, (5) a concert of a symphony orchestra, (6) an outdoor rock concert, or (7) a modern dance performance in a city park. Be sure to include all major production items, such as camera placement, audio and lighting requirements, intercom and transmission systems, power source, and so forth.

2. Prepare location sketches and facilities requests for the remote or EFP selected above.

3. You are the director for the live coverage of a large computer convention. While you're giving instructions to the talent to wind up her interview with one of the computer experts, her I.F.B. fails. How else can you communicate with her while she is on the air?

4. The producer learns at the last minute that the president of the European Union will arrive at the international airport and wants you to cover his arrival live. According to the producer, you should have no problem with the transmission because the station's transmitter is in line-of-sight of the airport. What field production method would you recommend? Specifically, what equipment and personnel would you need to accomplish this assignment?

5. To get a good overhead shot of a parade, you, the director, would like to place one of the cameras on the balcony of a twentieth-floor window of a nearby hotel. The TD informs you that the hotel manager has nothing against your renting the room for the day and setting up the camera, but she will not allow any cable runs either inside or outside the hotel. What would you suggest?

Scale: 1/4" = 1'

**Property List**

Scale: 1/4" = 1'

**Property List**

Scale: 1/4" = 1'

**Property List**

Scale: 1/4" = 1'

**Property List**